A colour guide to familiar
WOODLAND AND HILL
BIRDS

Eggs and Nests

By Jiří Felix

Illustrated by Květoslav Hísek

D0529918

octopus

Translated by Olga Kuthanová
Graphic design: Soňa Valoušková

This paperback edition first published 1983 by
Octopus Books Limited
59 Grosvenor Street, London W 1

Reprinted 1984, 1985, 1986, 1987

© 1974 Artia, Prague

ISBN 0 7064 1973 1

Printed in Czechoslovakia
3/10/06/51-11

CONTENTS

FOREWORD

Every nature lover welcomes a new book that will acquaint him with birds he does not yet know, and also provides a better knowledge of the more common species. If it helps him also to recognize their song and typical calls, their appearance in flight, the type of nest they build, the coloration of their eggs, as well as other interesting facts of their way of life, it becomes a valuable addition to his library.

This book describes birds of woodlands and mountain regions. Naturally, you may come across some of them in other, often quite different, environments. The cuckoo, for example, which is listed here as a woodland bird, is frequently found also in large reed beds bordering lakes or rivers.

Other birds such as the thrush and blackbird, living in built-up areas and not included in this book, are likewise common inhabitants of the woods, as are also some typical water birds such as the common heron, which often nests in woodlands if water is nearby.

This book is divided into three parts: a general introduction; texts to the individual pictures; and colour plates. In the first section the reader will learn about nesting, migration, hunting birds, falconry, the introduction of species from their native areas to new localities, the protection of woodland birds, etc. The text accompanying each colour plate gives the common and Latin names of the bird and acquaints the reader with its distribution, habitat, nest structure. It provides also a brief description of the bird, quoting its average length in centimetres, in some instances the wing span, call note, size of the egg and, if typical and helpful for identification, shows the flight silhouette.

The pictorial section is in two parts, depicting woodland birds and those of mountain areas. The latter group includes also birds found in mountain forests. In central Europe some species, for example the dotterel and redwing, occur only in the mountains, whereas in more northerly regions they are found in the tundra. The colour plates show the male (♂) of each species, but sometimes also the female (♀), together with the characteristic egg and, sometimes, a line drawing of the nest.

STRUCTURE OF THE BIRD

During their period of evolution, lasting several hundreds of thousands of years, birds became masters of the air. One of the main reasons was probably the fact that terrestrial animals posed no threat to their food supply. But with the passage of time some species reverted to life on the ground or in water, often losing entirely the ability to fly and becoming runners or swimmers.

For most birds, however, flight is the typical characteristic, and their degree of flight capability, as well as their flight silhouette, are important recognition factors, enabling even the layman to identify them at first glance as members of a specific group. The form of flight often differs greatly between species of birds and is allied to the general shape of their wings and wing surface. Birds capable of rapid and sustained flight have long, narrow, crescent-shaped wings (the swift and hobby), together with a slender body that offers minimum resistance to the air. The swift has evolved into such an efficient flying machine that it has poorly developed legs and is fairly helpless if grounded. They normally alight on ledges or posts and take off by dropping forward into the air. In complete contrast are the ground birds, such as those of the order *Gallinae*, of which pheasants are an example. They have fairly short, broad wings and plump bodies and, apart from a few exceptions, gallinaceous birds are indifferent fliers. They are able to take to the air quickly but can fly for only a very short distance. Consequently, they are usually resident birds and do not migrate. This does not mean that all large land birds cannot perform well in the air: some birds of prey, such as the buzzard and kestrel, can remain hovering in the air over a single spot for some time.

Each species of bird has also a typical flight silhouette, that is the shape or outline of the body, tail and wings when on the wing. Some, like the stork, swan and many more, fly with neck outstretched; others, such as the heron, carry it bent into an S.

The surface of a bird's body is covered with feathers, arranged in most species in definite tracts called *pteryla*. Only in some rare cases, such as the penguins, are the feathers distributed evenly over the entire body surface. The bare spaces between the feathered tracts are called *apteria*, but these are masked by the surrounding feathers. Those which give the body its typical shape are the outer flight and contour feathers, providing also some insulation. Beneath them is a layer of soft down which gives added insulation. Other types include filament or filoplume feathers, a degenerate feather with no known function, and bristle feathers. The latter are peculiar to a few birds such as the nightjar, the bristles around their mouth (gape) helping to catch insects during flight.

The strongest are the flight feathers, which are firm but flexible and serve to keep the bird airborne. Those at the tail serve to steer the bird on its course and maintain balanced flight. In some cases, such as the woodpecker, they serve also as a prop in climbing the trunks of trees or chipping out a hollow.

Most birds' feathers are shed and replaced regularly, this process being known as moulting. Old, worn feathers fall out as the new ones grow, and the wing quills and tail feathers are shed successively so that the bird does not lose its power of flight. Only in some species, ducks for example, are they shed all at one time, the birds thus going through a flightless period during which they remain concealed amidst reeds and rushes until new feathers grow in. But not all birds are subjects to complete moulting. Herons, bitterns and hawks have what are known as powder-down feathers which grow continuously, the tips of which disintegrate into a water-resistant powder used in preening.

Some birds don two differently coloured plumages in a year: the brightly coloured breeding plumage, especially in males, and the more sober non-breeding or winter plumage, usually more or less similar for both sexes. This change of coloration is characteristic of ducks, some shorebirds, finch-types and other birds.

In some species the male and female have the same coloration, the chiffchaff, tree creeper and tit being typical examples, while in others the colour of the male and sometimes the shape of various feathers are markedly different. Typical are the pheasant and capercaillie, this being known as sexual dimorphism.

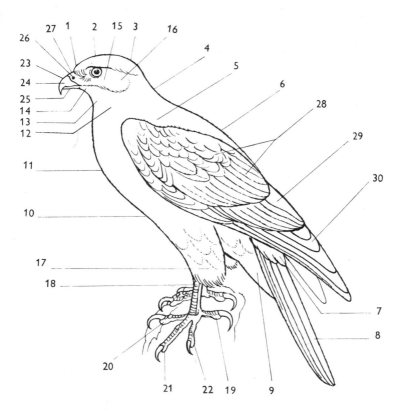

Bird topography: 1) forehead, 2) crown, 3) hind neck, 4) nape, 5) shoulder, 6) back, 7) upper tail coverts, 8) tail feathers, 9) under tail coverts, 10) belly, 11) breast, 12) neck, 13) throat, 14) chin, 15) cheek, 16) ear region, 17) thigh, 18) tarsus, 19) hind toe, 20) inner toe, 21) middle toe, 22) outer toe, 23) bill ridge, 24) upper mandible, 25) lower mandible, 26) nostril, 27) cere, 28) wing coverts, 29) secondaries, 30) primaries.

Some birds have so-called protective colouring that helps to conceal them from enemies. Thus, for example, the female pheasant, capercaillie and black grouse are sombrely coloured to escape the notice of predators, especially during the nesting period when the sitting hen is easy prey. Owls, too, have protective colouring, both males and females, for they have many enemies, especially in daylight. Birds of prey and corvines pursue owls if they see them during the day, and that is why owls are so drably coloured, often resembling the stump of a dead branch as they perch among the treetops.

Birds' feet have varied shapes, depending on the way of life of a given species. Tree creepers have toes with long, sharp claws that grip the bark as the bird climbs. Woodpeckers, too, have long, sharp claws that cut deep into the tree bark serving as an additional means of support to that provided by their strong tail feathers. The toes of woodpeckers are further adapted for climbing, two pointing forward and two backward. The feet of the nightjar are short with weak toes, making it almost impossible for the bird to move on the ground. It is also incapable of grasping a branch in the usual manner, which explains why it perches lengthwise and not crosswise. Birds of prey have huge claws on all four toes; those of eagles and hawks are extremely long, curved and sharp, whereas those of the vultures are straight and blunt, for these species have legs adapted to movement on the ground where they seek their food — carrion. Specially adapted are the toes of owls, with their long, sharply curved claws, the peculiarity in this case being that the outer toe may be directed forward, outward or completely backward, thus enabling the owl to catch its prey between opposite facing claws — a weapon few victims escape. One other predator, the osprey, has a reversible outer toe to facilitate catching fish under water, plus small spines on the pad of each toe to help in holding its slippery prey. Large, strong feet with blunt but strong claws are characteristic of the gallinaceous birds and serve to dig up seeds, insects and worms from the ground. And, of course, one must not overlook the webbed toes of the many birds that live and hunt primarily on and under water.

The shape of a bird's beak is also adapted for the function it serves, namely obtaining food. Thus, the bills of warblers are slender and slightly downcurved at the tip, so that they can easily catch small insects and their larvae. Flycatchers have a broad, flat and relatively wide bill, making it easier to catch insects in the air. The bill of thrushes resembles that of warblers but is stronger, for they eat larger insects, worms and also berries. Tits have a strong bill to break hard seed covering; tree creepers a long, downcurved bill that is very slender at the tip to help them extricate small insects, their eggs and larvae from cracks in the bark of trees. The bill of finch-type birds is stout and cone-shaped, useful in hulling seeds; that of the hawfinch, for instance, is unusually stout and enables it to crack even the hardest shells to get at the tender seeds and kernels inside. Crossbills, as their name indicates, have bills with overlapping tips to facilitate the extraction of seeds from the cones of conifers. Corvine birds, which are omnivorous, have an extremely large and stout bill. The nightjar, on the other hand, has a short but very wide bill with stiff bristles at the gape, which help it to catch insects on the wing. The bills of owls are downcurved and stout, testifying to their predatory way of life, the same as those of raptors, where the upper bills are not only downcurved but also have sharp edges that enable the birds to rip and tear the flesh of animals and to 'cut off' softer pieces. Some raptors, such as members of the family *Falconidae*, also have one or more horny 'teeth' in the upper bill, which further facilitates the tearing of flesh. Those of gallinaceous, or fowl-like, birds are comparatively short but very stout. In some species they are even shovel-shaped to facilitate turning of the earth in which the birds seek their food. Pigeons, too, have short bills with swollen ceres at the base, but with fairly hard tips which enable the pigeon to gather a variety of seeds and fruits. Woodpeckers have bills specially adapted for chiselling wood and uncovering concealed grubs.

INTERESTING FACTS ABOUT BIRDS

Migration

All birds found in present-day Europe are able to fly. Some are capable of rapid and sustained flight: others are clumsier and unable to remain airborne for long. Examples of these indifferent fliers are the gallinaceous birds, such as the capercaillie, pheasant and black grouse, which can get into the air quickly and fly for a short distance when danger threatens. This class of bird keeps close to its normal territory throughout the year. At the other end of the scale are the predators, birds that are the most skilful and fastest fliers of all, especially members of the *Falconidae* family. A hobby, for instance, can even catch a swallow or swift in the air, and these last two birds can fly at speeds of up to 160 kilometres per hour. But the hobby is able to attain a speed 20 kilometres per hour in excess of that. As for the peregrine falcon, plummeting downward to attack its prey with wings pressed close to the body, it can reach a speed of up to 280 kilometres per hour. The better fliers are all migratory birds, some of which travel hundreds and even thousands of kilometres each year in transit to and from their winter quarters.

Birds can be divided roughly into three groups according to whether they are migratory or not:

1. Resident birds — that never leave the general area of their nesting grounds, not even in winter.

2. Migratory birds — that leave their nesting grounds each year in late summer or early autumn, fly to warmer quarters for the winter and return again in the spring.

3. Transient migrants — birds that range far afield from their nesting grounds after the breeding season, often hundreds of kilometres.

There may, however, be various transitional stages between these three basic groups and, sometimes, contrary classification for members of one and the same species. For example, the peregrine falcon and kestrel which nest in northern Europe are migratory, whereas those of western and central Europe are resident. In other species, some members are migratory (mostly young birds and females) and others resident, namely males, as in the case of the blackbird. There are also species which, in general, are classed as migratory but some of their members remain in their nesting grounds for the winter; typical of this group are the robin and hedge sparrow.

Sometimes, however, birds that are otherwise resident will suddenly set out in large flocks on a long journey south or southwest; these are called invasional migrations. One example is the nutcracker, normally a resident or transient migrant, which sometimes, however, travels in large flocks to central Europe from the north or northeast. There are also the birds which became regular winter guests, migrants who have left their breeding grounds in the far north to spend the winter in central or western Europe.

Most birds in Europe migrate in roughly three main directions: from north and northwest across western Europe and the Iberian Peninsula; from north and central Europe southward across Italy and Sicily to northwest Africa; and from northeast Europe across the Balkan Peninsula and Asia Minor. There may, of course, be deviations from these routes and it is not uncommon for birds of the same species, but different populations, to travel in different directions. Many migratory birds of central Europe travel west or southwest as a rule, spending the winter no farther afield than southwest Europe or northwest Africa. One such example is the mistle thrush, although individual members inhabiting western and southern Europe remain resident. Redwings from the north winter in western or southern Europe, and the wood pigeon is to be found in southwest Europe, France and Spain.

Some European birds fly as far as tropical and southern Africa. This is an almost unbelievable distance of more than ten thousand kilometres, which they travel twice each year, in spring and autumn. Thus we find that the honey buzzard winters in tropical Africa, as do the flycatcher, chiffchaff and oriole. The nightjar journeys as far as eastern and southern Africa and our old friend the cuckoo has its winter quarters in tropical and southern Africa. South and west Africa is host to the hobby during the winter, whereas its larger relative, the peregrine falcon, journeys no further than western and south-western Europe. This is true, of course, of individuals from Europe's northerly regions; peregrine falcons from other parts of Europe are either resident or transient migrants.

The autumn migration of falcons begins in October and is a leisurely affair, as is often the case of other migratory birds. Falcons often stop for a few days in towns where pigeons nest in great numbers, attacking them from church towers and other vantage points which serve as their temporary quarters. Similar winter areas are visited by Europe's smallest predator of the *Falconidae* family, the merlin, which regularly crosses central Europe on its journey from Scandinavia en route to places as far distant as northwest Africa. The honey buzzard makes even longer flights, as far as tropical west Africa, while the rough-legged buzzard, *Buteo lagopus*, which nests in the far northern tundras, passes the winter in central Europe.

Typical residents are the gallinaceous birds of Europe, with the exception of the quail. Some tits, woodpeckers and owls, especially the horned owl, are mostly resident but may some-times travel southwest. This is not true migration. Corvine birds are mostly transient migrants.

Migratory birds do not make the journey to their winter quarters without a break. This would be an impossible task. They usually fly about 60 to 100 kilometres a day, though shorebirds hold the record, sometimes covering between 300 to 600 kilometres a day. After a short time to rest and find food they set off again; if the weather is bad, however, they remain for several days in one place. The return passage to the nesting grounds is faster, usually by about a third, for the birds are urged on by the breeding instinct. The average air speed of a bird on migratory flights is less than that of which it is capable over short distances, as when fleeing from an enemy or attacking prey. Thus, the rook flies at about 50 kilometres per hour, the finch 52 kilometres and the sparrow up to 70 kilometres. Some migrating birds fly only during the day (swallows and finches), others only at night (warblers and chiffchaffs). There are also those like thrushes and wagtails which show no particular preference and fly by night or day, the actual flying time being limited to only a few hours in each twenty-four.

The Bird Family

Arrival at the nesting grounds is usually the signal for the beginning of the courtship display though, in some species, this may have started already in the birds' winter quarters or during the return journey.

The males' behaviour is marked by agitation and excitement as they try to attract a partner. Each species has its characteristic manner of courtship: in some it is fairly inconspicuous while in others it is quite noticeable, often including intricate antics and loud cries.

The courtship display may take place on the ground, among the branches of trees, as well as in the air and on water. In some species several males participate in the display simultaneously and even engage in duels. Among woodland birds the black grouse provides a good example, the males of the species converging in a single open space for a mass display. The capercaillie, on the other hand, performs its antics at a higher level, usually on tree branches, and the ceremony consists of several stages. The courtship display of cooing pigeons is also quite distinctive; they bow and strut about, or hop along and drag their wings along the ground. The male pheasant stands on the ground, stretches its neck upward and rapidly whirs its wings, at the same time emitting trumpet-like sounds that can be heard from a great distance. When courting the males of most songbirds sing, while other species produce unusual sounds. Woodpeckers, for instance, select that part of a tree which has good resonance and drum on it with their strong bills.

The courtship display of a number of species of birds includes spectacular flights. This is especially the case with the raptors, which sometimes perform fantastic acrobatic feats. These aerial displays begin when the bird circles to gain height, then plummets downwards only to soar up high again, making all kinds of turns and somersaults and providing a magnificent display of its flying skill and artistry.

Prior to nesting, birds stake out a specific area called the nesting ground or territory. The boundaries of this area are jealously guarded and defended by the male of the species. Once the territories have become established they are usually respected by the males of other species. The size of the nesting ground varies according to the amount of food available in the area and, in the case of birds which nest in tree cavities and the like, the abundance of nesting sites. Small songbirds have a fairly small nesting area, embracing a radius of some 40 to 70 metres from the nest. Larger songbirds, like the crow and jay, have much bigger territories, while large raptors may require an area covering as much as several square kilometres.

In this context, however, it should be understood that one nesting ground may be inhabited by several pairs of different species, birds that feed on different food and therefore are not rivals. Some species are colonial nesters, groups of birds foraging for food in outlying areas so that the nesting territory is limited only to the actual nest and its immediate vicinity.

When a male songbird stakes out his territory he announces it to all and sundry by his characteristic song; woodpeckers drum on a tree trunk with their beak; pheasants have a special call note; many birds of prey emit a sharp cry and male cuckoos sound their 'cuckoo' note. In each case the message is clear: this area is mine.

Before nesting, birds usually build a new nest in which the hen lays the eggs. Some species, especially songbirds, build complex nests that are almost works of art. It is often possible to determine the species of a bird by the shape of its nest, for the method of construction is a trait which is inherited, and, as a rule, a particular species will always use the same building materials. Buntings, for example, build their nests with stems of grass and horsehair. Some birds, such as woodpeckers, hollow out cavities in tree trunks, while others look for a ready-made cavity. Included in this group are tits, flycatchers, nuthatches and even certain owls and birds of prey, like the kestrel. Some owls, on the other hand, seek out the abandoned nests of raptors, such as crows and herons. Other birds, like the woodcock, nest on the ground in a small depression lined lightly with leaves and some, like the nightjar, lay their eggs directly on the ground without any lining at all.

Each species produces eggs which have characteristic coloration and shape although some, like the cuckoo, lay eggs which show a marked variation. In the case of many songbirds, such as the flycatcher, chiffchaff, tit and wren, the eggs are incubated by the hen alone. In the case of pigeons, woodpeckers, certain raptors and some songsters they are incubated by both partners. Sometimes it is only the male that incubates the eggs and attends to the young; the dotterel is one such example amongst European birds.

Birds whose young have to be fed and cared for by the parents for some period after hatching are called *nidicolous* species. This category includes songbirds, woodpeckers, pigeons, owls and raptors. Those whose young are capable of independent activity from birth are called *nidifugous* species. Fowl-like species such as the pheasant, caparcaillie and black grouse are representatives of this group.

The young of songbirds and woodpeckers generally have no feathers when they hatch, whereas those of owls and raptors are covered with a thick layer of down. As a rule the young of the *nidicolous* species are fed by both parents, but in the case of some raptors, such as the sparrowhawk, goshawk and falcon, the male hunts for the food and it is portioned and fed to the young by the female. In such families if a hen with young nestlings dies, the cock is unable to rear the family because he does not know how. Only the larger nestlings survive, namely those capable of tearing the prey that the male brings to the nest. The hobby is of particular interest in this respect in that the male follows this procedure with prey such as birds, but if he catches small insects will often feed the young himself.

Vultures feed their nestlings partially digested food, regurgitated from the crop into the bill.

The young of smaller types of songbirds remain in the nest for a period of twelve days before fledging, while those of larger songsters, such as the jackdaw, remain for about a month As a rule the parent birds continue to feed the young for a further two to three weeks after they have left the nest. The young of many species, thrush-types being a typical example, leave the nest before they are capable of flight and scatter in the neighbourhood, concealing themselves in the vegetation where the parents are compelled to seek them out to feed them. This strange behaviour on the part of both young and parent birds has evolved as a protective measure to prevent vermin from destroying all the occupants of a nest. It is clearly more difficult to catch all of the scattered nestlings. The young of other, larger birds remain in the nest for about one month; those of large raptors such as vultures stay for up to three or four months.

The young of *nidifugous* species are capable of feeding themselves from the very first day of hatching. However, they venture forth only under the guidance of the parent birds and conceal themselves beneath the shelter of their wings during the night or in inclement weather, where they find not only a warm haven but also partial protection from vermin. The parents, usually just the hen, also lead their young to places where there is an abundant supply of food which the chicks can gather on their own.

Small songbirds, who often have large families to feed during the nesting period, seek food only in the immediate vicinity of the nest. Species that feed young less frequently, and obtain larger quantities at a time, often range a distance of several kilometres. This is true of raptors which fly far from the nest in search of large prey that will satisfy the entire family for some time. The golden eagle, which weighs an average of 4.5 kilograms, often returns with a piece weighing up to seven kilograms — a truly remarkable feat.

Naturally such a catch is exceptional and may represent a two-day supply of food for the whole family. As a rule the prey is much smaller.

SOCIAL PARASITES

One unusual facet of social behaviour which is found only amongst birds, is their habit of depositing their eggs in the nests of other species. After hatching the nestlings are raised by the foster parents often at the cost of their own young.

In Europe the most typical example of the social parasite is the cuckoo. The main distribution area of the cuckoo is the tropics and not all cuckoos behave like parasites; most build their own nests and incubate the young themselves. Nevertheless cuckoos have acquired a reputation as intruders into the homes of other birds, even though there are other parasites amongst exotic species.

In all probability this habit originated as the result of the indiscriminate laying of eggs by two different hens in one and the same nest. Over a period of time it has evolved into the parasitism of whole populations and, finally, of entire species. In the case of many birds two or more females of the same species lay their eggs in one nest. The eggs are then incubated and the young reared by just one pair of adults. This, however, is not true social parasitism.

Let us take a closer look at the common cuckoo *(Cuculus canorus)*, the best known of the social parasites. It is found throughout Europe and practically the whole of Asia, up to the tree line at the borders of the taiga, as well as in northwest Africa and in some places south of the Sahara. European cuckoos and those of the species from northwest Africa winter south of the Sahara; Asian populations winter in India and southeast Asia, including the islands of Indonesia. Cuckoos living in Africa, south of the Sahara, are resident.

European cuckoos fly south very early, many leaving their breeding grounds in the second half of July. The main mass flight, however, takes place in August. The older birds are the first to leave and young cuckoos depart much later; they are often seen in central Europe even in late September. With the onset of March the cuckoos begin the return trip to their northern breeding grounds, usually arriving in central Europe at the end of April or the beginning of May.

First to appear at the nesting territory are the males, followed a few days later by the females. The male generally returns to the same place as in previous years, and one bird was observed to do so for thirty-two years. Females also return as a rule to their old nesting territory and on their arrival the male attracts the attention of the female with his cries and display, which includes spreading his tail feathers, drooping his wings, ruffling his body feathers and stretching his neck forward while he utters his characteristic cuckoo call. This is usually done early in the morning or towards evening.

The size of the territory depends on the number of songbirds nesting there, for the female cuckoo usually deposits her eggs in their nests. As a rule, the territory embraces an area of about 1—1½ kilometres in diameter. Though a regular denizen of the woods, when it comes to selecting a nesting site the cuckoo shows no particular preference for vegetation. The cuckoo may be found wherever there is an abundance of nests and this, apparently, is its main consideration during the breeding season.

As a rule the female cuckoo lays her eggs in the nests of the species that she herself was reared by. The mere sight of a partially built nest arouses the laying instinct in the hen, but if there are few such nests in the territory, this instinct is suppressed. The female flies around looking for a suitable nest, preferably one which contains a clutch of eggs. As soon as she finds one, she waits until the adult birds depart, then quickly lays her egg there, removing one or sometimes several of the foster parents' eggs, either by casting them to the ground or by swallowing them. The cuckoo generally lays from fifteen to twenty eggs in one breeding season.

It has been found that cuckoos deposit their eggs in the nests of 162 different species of birds, though usually the choice is limited to some twenty species of small songsters. Cuckoo eggs are very small but have a much thicker shell than those of other birds. This is to prevent them from breaking when they are dropped from a fair height into the nest or cavity.

Birds that have been 'selected' by the cuckoo as foster parents for its young often cannot suffer the cuckoo's presence in the vicinity of their nest and try to chase it away. If the cuckoo does manage to lay an egg in their nest many birds simply throw it out, while others abandon the nest and build a new one. Warblers and redstarts simply cover the whole clutch, including the cuckoo's egg, with a new lining and lay a fresh batch of eggs. Not all birds behave like this; there are a great number who hatch the eggs and rear the young cuckoos.

How some birds do and others do not recognize the danger posed to their species by the cuckoo's egg is something that still remains to be explained adequately. The cuckoo nestling generally hatches sooner than the young of its foster parents since it has a shorter period of incubation than most songbirds. The young cuckoo is completely naked at birth and hatches with closed eyes. However, some ten to sixteen hours later it instinctively feels the need to remove from the nest anything which gets in its way. The skin of the young cuckoo's back is extremely sensitive to contact with foreign objects. It puts its head and neck under the object, spreads its feet wide and rests its head against the bottom of the nest. It then lifts the object onto its back, holding it in place with its stumpy wings, and pushes it towards the edge of the nest until it tumbles out. The process continues until all the eggs or the young nestlings of the foster parents have been cast from the nest. This instinct remains active for three to four days, by which time the young cuckoo is the sole occupant of the nest and receives the foster parents' full attention. It consumes enough food for a whole family of small songbirds and grows very rapidly, especially during the first two to nine days.

When it hatches the young cuckoo's cry resembles that of most songbird nestlings, and it is not till the fifth day that it changes to the typical cry of cuckoo nestlings demanding food. Because its gullet is a bright orange colour, its open beak continually implores the foster parents to hasten with the feeding. The cuckoo's diet consists mainly of fruits, beetles, butterflies and various caterpillars, even the hairy varieties; the hairs of such caterpillars become embedded in the walls of the bird's stomach and are regurgitated, together with the lining which is 'shed' regularly.

The cuckoo nestling remains in the nest for twenty to twenty-three days, after which it climbs out and perches on a branch, though still unable to fly, and is fed by the foster parents for a further three to four weeks.

The plates depict 64 species of birds. In those cases where the coloration of the male differs from that of the female (sexual dimorphism) both are shown. Also included is a colour illustration of the typical egg of the given species and sometimes a pen-and-ink drawing of the nest. The plates are arranged according to the birds' biotopes and within each group according to the zoological system of classification. The text accompanying each plate gives the basic biological data about the given species as well as items of particular interest. The column at top right gives the average length of the bird in centimetres, measured from the tip of the bill to the tip of the tail, the bird's coloration, a verbal description of the song and dimensions of the egg. These dimensions are given in millimetres, e.g. 15.5−19.5×12.0−14.4 mm, the first figure denoting the minimum length of the egg, the second the maximum length, the third the minimum width and the fourth the maximum width.

Pied Flycatcher
Ficedula hypoleuca

The black and white male pied flycatcher is quite common in thin woods from as early as the beginning of April. He flies impatiently from one tree to another, seeking a nesting cavity suitable for raising a family. His choice is generally an abandoned woodpecker's nest, though a man-made nest box is also welcomed. The soberly coloured female then lines the nest selected by the male in a hollow shape with quantities of silky moss brought in her slender beak and further lines it with soft animal hairs. From the middle of May until June she then lays from 5 to 8 eggs, which she herself incubates for 13 to 15 days. The male helps feed the young with small insects, which the parent birds capture on the wing, as well as small caterpillars and spiders. The nestlings leave the nest at the age of 14 to 16 days, but continue to be fed by the parents for a further two weeks or so. After the young have fledged the whole family roams the countryside around the nest and, in late August or early September, sets out on the long journey to tropical Africa. The pied flycatcher inhabits most of Europe, except Italy and Ireland, and also northwest and southwest Germany and western France, where it is seen only during the migrating season. Otherwise it is found only in certain regions, and in some areas only nests sporadically. Its distribution is irregular, being abundant in some places while in others it is rare.

Length: 13 cm. The male's non-breeding plumage resembles the female's, but he has a white forehead.
Voice: A short 'whit'.
Song: Clear 'zee-it zee-it zee-it' sounds.
Size of Egg: 15.5—19.5 × 12.0—14.4 mm.

Willow Warbler

Phylloscopus trochilus

Sylviidae

The loud rippling song of the willow warbler can be heard in April when it returns from its winter quarters in tropical and southern Africa, in thick deciduous or mixed woods with thick undergrowth, less often in coniferous forests. It is a small bird and is distributed throughout Europe, except the southern parts and the Balkans, though in the east its range extends as far as northeast Siberia. It hops about and flits restlessly from branch to branch, collecting small insects and their larvae, as well as small spiders. In the warm days of May or June the female builds a neat dome-shaped nest in a clump of grass, or close above the ground in a blueberry bush or heather. The nest is made of grass stems, dead leaves, moss and lichens and lined with fine materials. The entrance is located at the side so that the clutch is out of sight. The 6 to 7 eggs are incubated by the hen alone, usually for 13 days, but the male helps share the duties of rearing the young. They leave the nest after 12 to 16 days, but continue to be fed by the parents for a further 14 days. The diet consists mainly of small insects and their larvae. The cuckoo often lays its eggs in the willow warbler's nest, and on hatching the young cuckoo is often reared by the willow warblers and fed by them for far longer than their own nestlings. In September or October the willow warbler leaves the nesting grounds for its winter quarters. It is one of the most plentiful species of woodland birds.

Length: 11 cm. The male and female have like plumage.
Voice: A bright 'hooeet'.
Song: Resembling that of the chaffinch but a softer and more rippling 'sooeet-sooeetoo'.
Size of Egg: 13.2—18.8 × 10.9—13.8 mm.

Wood Warbler
Phylloscopus sibilatrix

The wood warbler is found throughout Europe as far as western Siberia, with the exception of Spain, Portugal, Ireland and Scandinavia. By the end of April or the beginning of May, this small bird returns from its winter haunts in tropical Africa to its nesting grounds in thin deciduous or mixed woods in lowland as well as hilly country. It may also be found in coniferous forests, but only in such places where there is the occasional broad-leaved tree and thick undergrowth. The round covered nest with a fairly large side entrance is built by the female on the ground in a tussock. It is a fairly large structure considering the bird's small dimensions, and the side entrance is far larger than those in the nests of other warblers. By the end of May or beginning of June the nest already contains the full clutch of 5 to 7 eggs, which are incubated by the hen alone. The young hatch after 12 days and are fed by both parents, the mainstay of the diet being insects and their larvae. These are gathered mostly from deciduous trees and the undergrowth. The young become fledged at the age of 12 days. The wood warbler can be easily identified by its typical chattering song. It also differs from other warblers in having a bright yellow throat and breast and a broad stripe above the eye; these features, however, can be recognized in the wild only with the aid of powerful field glasses. Between the end of August and the middle of September the wood warbler leaves its breeding grounds and sets out on its journey for Africa, where it spends the winter months.

Length: 13 cm. The male and female have like plumage.
Voice: 'Pru' or 'whit whit whit'.
Song: Chattering, beginning with a repeated 'piu', followed by a lengthy 'stip stip stip' and ending with 'shreeee'.
Size of Egg: 14.0—18.3 ×11.4—13.5 mm.

Goldcrest

Regulidae

Regulus regulus

The goldcrest, smallest of European birds (it weighs only 5 to 6 grams), inhabits most of Europe except Iceland and the northernmost parts of Scandinavia. In Spain it is found only in the central parts of the country. It may be seen in pine and spruce woods, from lowland to mountain elevations up to the tree line. In winter it sometimes appears also in parks. Though mostly a resident bird, some individuals from northern localities travel to southern or western Europe in winter. During the winter months flocks of goldcrests flit about in the treetops. At the end of April, and often for a second time in June, pairs of goldcrests weave a fairly large structure of small twigs, stalks, moss, lichen, spiders' webs and hairs. The round nest, narrowing at the top, is carefully concealed in the thick branches of coniferous trees and, when viewed from above, appears to be closed except for a very tiny opening. There is good reason for this, for goldcrests must hide from their enemies — jays and other predators as well as squirrels and dormice — which often plunder their nests. The 8 to 11 eggs are incubated by the hen for 14 to 16 days. The young are fed small caterpillars, spiders and flies by both parents. When they are about 14 days old the young leave the nest and pass the night in the thick branches of a tree together with their parents. In winter the goldcrest feeds on insect eggs and cocoons it collects from tree branches. It is a very active bird with a good appetite.

Length: 9 cm. The female has a yellow crest.
Voice: A soft 'zee-zee-zee' or louder 'whit'.
Song: Composed of similar tones.
Size of Egg: 12.1—14.6 ×9.2—11.0 mm.

Mistle Thrush

Turdus viscivorus

The mistle thrush, the herald of spring, arrives at its breeding grounds sometimes as early as the end of February. It is distributed throughout all Europe, except Iceland; its range extends also to northwest Africa, the Middle East and western Asia. Individuals from western and southern Europe remain there the year round, being joined in October and November by populations from other parts of Europe that have come to winter there. The mistle thrush is found in coniferous and mixed woods, at lowland as well as mountain elevations, and in western Europe frequents parks. It generally builds its nest high in the forks of trees at the end of March and a second time in June. The nest is constructed of twigs, grass, roots and moss and is lined with a layer of mud and fine grasses. The task is performed by the female, though the male also helps, bringing the necessary construction materials. The 4 to 5 eggs are incubated by the hen alone, for a period of about 14 days. The young leave the nest at the age of 14 to 16 days, though still incapable of flight. In the autumn these birds roam the countryside, migrant populations usually flying southwest. The mistle thrush generally seeks its food at the edges of forests or in forest clearings. The diet consists of insects, worms, small molluscs, and fruits and berries in the autumn. In spring the mistle thrush flies to the tops of tall conifers, where it delivers its loud song. At one time it was a popular game bird but now is a protected species.

Length: 26.5 cm. The male and female have like plumage.
Voice: A hard 'tuc-tuc-tuc' and a thin 'see-ip'.
Song: Resembling that of the blackbird but louder and with pauses between individual phrases.
Size of Egg: 25.8—35.8 ×19.6—24.4 mm.

eldfare

urdus pilaris

Northern Europe is the home of the fieldfare, one of the few songbirds that were once important and prized game birds. It was hunted mostly during the migrating season and its meat was considered a great delicacy. Today, however, it is no longer hunted in most European countries. The fieldfare nests in many parts of central Europe, which it has been invading from the north in increasing numbers since the end of the nineteenth century. In some of these parts it breeds regularly and in fair abundance. Fieldfares return to their breeding grounds in flocks at the end of March, nesting together in small colonies in woods, parks and thickets alongside brooks and ponds, as well as in thin birch or pine groves. There the individual pairs build nests close to one another in thickets, or in trees 2 to 10 metres above the ground; as a rule they are located at a height of 3 metres, though in the tundra they are only 30 to 50 centimetres above the ground. The nest is made of dry twigs, roots and stems with a small amount of mud and lined with fine stems. The clutch comprises 4 to 6 eggs and these are incubated, primarily by the hen, for 13 to 14 days, the young leaving the nest after the same period of time. The fieldfare feeds on insects, worms, small molluscs, beetles and caterpillars: in the autumn and winter months mostly on berries such as rowanberry. In October fieldfares from the north arrive in large flocks to spend the winter in central, western and southern Europe.

Length: 25.5 cm. The male and female have like plumage. Conspicuous in flight is the white belly and underside of the wings.
Voice: A loud 'tchak-tchak-tchak', also 'see see'.
Song: Semi-loud and pleasant.
Size of Egg: 25.0—33.5 × 19.0—23.4 mm.

Redwing

Turdus iliacus

The redwing is a typical thrush of northern Europe and Asia. In rare instances it also nests in central Europe in colder mountain areas near mountain streams. During its migration in the winter months it occurs in abundance in central Europe on its way to its winter quarters in western and southern Europe, or as far south as northwest Africa. At this time it forms large flocks that alight in beech and mountain ash woods to feed on rowanberries. Sometimes it joins flocks of fieldfares, some pairs staying with them even during the nesting period.

Between the middle of March and the beginning of April the redwing returns to its breeding grounds, in thin birch woods as well as coniferous forests with thick undergrowth and, in Scandinavia, also in larger parks. Their nests are found in deciduous and coniferous trees at a height of about 3 metres, in tundras only 30 to 50 centimetres above the ground, and sometimes even on the ground. Made of dry twigs, roots, plant stalks and mud, it is plastered inside with a layer of mud mixed with mucous secretions. The female lays 4 to 6 eggs from May to July, which both birds take turns incubating for 13 to 15 days. The young are fed mostly on insects and their larvae by the adult birds for 11 to 14 days in the nest, plus a further three weeks after fledging. When the young have fledged the redwings gather in flocks, which set out on their southward journey at the end of October or the beginning of November.

Length: 21 cm. The male and female have like plumage.
Voice: 'Tchack tchack', when alarmed also 'terr terr', at night and in flight a clear 'see-ip'.
Song: 4 flute-like tones interspersed with chattering and rasping sounds.
Size of Egg: 22.0—29.1 × 17.2—20.7 mm.

∍bin *Turdidae*

rithacus rubecula

Deciduous, mixed and coniferous woods with thick undergrowth from lowland to mountain elevations are the home of the robin in practically the whole of Europe, except Iceland and northern Scandinavia. Its range extends eastward as far as western Siberia and it is also found in northwest Africa. In western and central Europe it is plentiful in parks and cemeteries, preferring thickly overgrown, dimly lighted spots, which accounts for its conspicuously large eyes. Northern and eastern populations migrate in September and October and winter in western and parts of southern Europe and north Africa. They often fly to England in the autumn, facilitating their journey by 'catching a ride' on ships crossing the channel. In recent years central Europe has had its share of adult males staying the winter, feeding on various berries. March marks the return of the birds to their breeding grounds, where in April the females begin building their nests of roots, plant stalks and moss. These are well concealed between stones, under protruding roots, in piles of underbrush, less frequently in a hollow stump, and are lined with thin roots, fine plant parts and sometimes with animal hairs. The 3 to 6 eggs are incubated only by the hen for a period of 13 to 14 days, but the male assists her in feeding the young with insects, larvae and spiders. The young leave the nest at the age of 12 to 15 days, though as yet incapable of flight, and conceal themselves on the ground where the parents bring them food.

Length: 14 cm.
The female resembles the male but is not as brightly coloured.
Voice: A ringing 'tic' or 'tsip'.
Song: Loud and melodious.
The male sings perched in a tree.
Size of Egg:
16.9—22.2
× 13.8—16.3 mm.

Wren

Troglodytes troglodytes

The wren, one of the smallest European birds (it weighs only 8 to 9 grams), makes its home in woods throughout most of Europe. It is also found in parts of Asia, northwest Africa and north America. This agile and restless bird remains in its breeding grounds throughout the year; only individuals from the north travel south for the winter. Its favourite habitat is woods with thick undergrowth, though it also likes thickets alongside ponds, ditches and streams. It is sometimes found in parks and, in winter, frequently enters villages. It also enjoys digging around in piles of underbrush, where it can usually find something to eat. In spring the male stakes out his nesting territory which he stoutly defends and, at the end of April, he begins building several nests, which are made of plant stalks, small twigs and moss and provided with a tiny side entrance. The female then examines the results of his efforts, selecting the one she considers best, and it is then lined with animal hairs and feathers. The nests are located in the branches of spruce trees, stacks of wood, between roots, in piles of brushwood and similar sites, and the ones not chosen by the female are used by the male as sleeping quarters. The hen incubates the 5 to 7 eggs alone for 14 to 16 days and 15 to 17 days after that the young leave the nest. In June the parent birds often have a second brood, the male taking the first brood to roost in one of the rejected nests while the female is occupied with incubation. The wren's diet consists of insects, insect larvae, spiders and small seeds.

Length: 9.5 cm. The male and female have like plumage.
Voice: A loud 'tit-tit-tit', and twittering 'tserr'.
Song: Loud and heard often, even in winter.
Size of Egg: 14.7—18.9 ×11.5—13.5 mm.

Coal Tit

Paridae

arus ater

The coal tit is a bird of tall but not very deep coniferous forests, from lowland to mountain elevations, distributed throughout the whole of Europe except the northernmost parts. Its range extends eastward as far as Kamchatka and southern China and it is found also in northwest Africa. It prefers pine woods but is plentiful also in spruce stands. In some parts of Great Britain and Ireland it may also be found in mixed woods and in the mountain areas of southern Europe among beechwoods. Individuals from central, western and southern Europe are resident as a rule, whereas populations from eastern and northern Europe migrate in vast numbers to central Europe for the winter. Such journeys, however, are not undertaken regularly. At the end of April the coal tit builds its nest of moss in a tree cavity; if there is a scarcity of these it will use hollow tree stumps, ground burrows, or rock crevices, lining the inside with hairs. It would also welcome a nesting box. The female lays 7 to 11 eggs, which she alone incubates for a period of 14 to 15 days, rarely a day more or less. The young are fed insects, insect larvae and spiders by both parents. They leave the nest at the age of 16 to 17 days, but continue to be fed by the adult birds for another two weeks. Having reared one brood the coal tit has a second, usually in July. Following the nesting period the birds form flocks, roaming the woods of the surrounding countryside together with other tits, generally passing the night singly in tree cavities.

Length: 11 cm. The male and female have like plumage.
Voice: In spring the characteristic 'seetoo seetoo seetoo', the courting call a soft 'sissi-sissi-sissi', and a scolding 'chi-chi-chich'.
Size of Egg: 13.3—16.8 × 10.5—12.1 mm.

Crested Tit

Paridae

Parus cristatus

The lovely crested tit is plentiful throughout Europe but absent from England, Ireland, Italy and the far north. It makes its home in tall evergreen forests from lowland to mountain elevations, though in western Europe, interestingly enough, it is occurring with increasing frequency also in deciduous woods, where it finds more cavities suitable for nesting. During the courting season in spring the male spreads and closes his head-crest and executes various bows while he sings his 'serenade'. He often has trouble finding a suitable cavity in which to build his nest and sometimes has to be satisfied with an abandoned squirrel's drey, an old overturned tree stump or a man-made nest box. On occasion, though rarely, he excavates his own hole in rotten wood. The female lays the first clutch of 7 to 10 eggs in April, incubating them herself for 15 to 18 days. The young, which leave the nest after 20 to 22 days, are fed by both parents. When they have fledged the parent birds generally have a second brood in June, often using the same nest. In the autumn months the crested tits join groups of other tits, often acting as leaders of the flock when it roams the countryside in winter. Their diet consists mainly of small insects, especially aphids, bark beetles and weevils and, in winter, various seeds. The crested tit is adroit at squeezing between the thick branches of conifers in search of food and if it does not find enough there it often seeks fallen seeds on the ground.

Length: 11.5 cm.
The male and female have like plumage.
Voice:
The characteristic 'tzee tzee tzee', often only 'choo-r-r'.
Size of Egg:
14.3—17.8 ×11.8—13.3 mm.

** low Tit** *Paridae*

us montanus

The willow tit makes its home in damp evergreen forests, in lesser numbers also in mixed woods, both in lowland country and mountain areas. It is distributed throughout most of Europe, except Spain, Ireland and Italy. It generally remains throughout the winter, though individuals from the north occasionally form large flocks and travel to central and southern Europe. This does not happen regularly and is not considered as true migration. The willow tit's range extends eastward as far as Japan and it is found also in North America. Pairs of these birds stay together permanently, even after the breeding season, forming flocks that roam the countryside. In spring the female laboriously excavates a hole for her nest in a rotten tree stump. The male does not assist in this task, which often takes more than three weeks. If the wood is well rotted the hole can be excavated in about two weeks. Often, however, the female avails herself of a natural cavity. In May she lays 6 to 9 eggs, which she incubates alone for 14 days. The task of feeding the young, however, is shared by both partners — 17 to 18 days in the nest and a further two weeks after the nestlings have fledged. The parent birds make about twenty trips an hour, bringing caterpillars, aphids, flies, small beetles and spiders. After the young have fledged the birds roam the countryside far and wide in search of food. In winter they feed also on the seeds of various conifers, collecting them on the ground. The willow tit is on the move the whole day long, only stopping now and then for a brief rest.

Length: 11.5 cm. The male and female have like plumage.
Voice: Courting and alarm note a repeated 'eez-eez-eez' with a short 'zi-zi-zi' in between. The male also makes a loud 'day' sound.
Size of Egg: 14.4—16.3 ×11.8—12.4 mm.

Nuthatch

Sitta europaea

Sittidae

The nuthatch is a common bird of thin deciduous, mixed and coniferous woods, as well as parks and large gardens. It is found throughout all of Europe, except Ireland and northern Scandinavia. It is a resident bird, remaining in its breeding grounds throughout the winter, when it may often be seen in the vicinity of houses, where it visits window-box feeders. Sunflower seeds are its favourite food. Picking one up in its beak it will fly off with it to a nearby branch, where it wedges it in the bark, cracks the seed coat and swallows the kernel, after which it flies back again to the feeder for another. In spring, either at the end of April or the beginning of May, the female lays 6 to 10 eggs in tree cavities lined with pine bark chips or dead leaves. The nuthatch will often venture several hundred metres from the nest. If the entrance is too large the female narrows it by plastering the edges of the hole with small pellets of mud mixed with mucous secretions, which she then smooths with her beak. The eggs are incubated by the hen alone for 13 to 14 days, but both parents share the duties of feeding the young. The male sleeps in another cavity nearby, having first ensured that his mate is comfortably settled for the night. The young leave the nest after 22 to 24 days and soon learn to clamber up and down tree trunks with great adroitness, like their parents, hunting insects and spiders in the bark, often head downwards. In winter they also feed on seeds, which they often store in cracks.

Length: 14 cm. The male and female have like plumage. The young are greyer.
Voice: In early spring a loud whistling that sounds like 'chwit-chwit-chwit', courting note 'tsit-tsit', or a long trilling 'chi-chi-chi' or 'qui-qui-qui-qui'.
Size of Egg: 17.2—22.5 × 13.5—15.4 mm.

Tree Creeper

Certhiidae

Certhia familiaris

The tree creeper is an inconspicuous bird with a long, slightly downcurved bill, which it uses to collect small insects, their eggs, larvae and pupae from crevices in the bark of trees. Like the nuthatch and woodpecker it also climbs trees, but travels upwards and around the trunk in a spiral, using its tail as a prop. It is found chiefly in coniferous forests from lowland to mountain elevations, but occurs also in mixed and sometimes even in deciduous woods. Except for southwestern Europe and northern Scandinavia, it is widespread throughout the Continent, extending eastward as far as Japan and occurring also in North and Central America. It does not leave its nesting grounds even in the most severe winters, flitting about in the woods in search of food. In the middle of April it builds its nest under a piece of loose bark, in crannies, piles of wood and other semi-cavities. The nest is woven of dried grass, rootlets, lichens and moss on a layer of small dry twigs, and lined with a thick layer of feathers and hairs. The 5 to 7 eggs are incubated by the hen for a period of 13 to 15 days. Whether the male aids her in this task is not yet known with sufficient certainty. The nestlings are fed by both parents with small insects and their larvae, as well as spiders. The young leave the nest after 15 to 16 days, being fed by the adult birds for a short while longer. Often the tree creeper has a second brood, usually in June. The young birds roam the neighbourhood and the following year raise their own families there.

Length: 12.5 cm. The male and female have like plumage.
Voice: Sounds resembling 'tsee' or 'tsit' but uttered only rarely.
Song: Resembling the trill of the blue tit and also similar to the song of the wren.
Size of Egg: 14.0—16.7 ×11.0—13.0 mm.

Hawfinch

Fringillidae

Coccothraustes coccothraustes

The hawfinch makes its home in thin deciduous woods from lowland to mountain elevations, as well as in large parks and gardens. Its most marked characteristic is the enormous parrot-shaped beak, with which it can crack hard seeds, cherry stones and the like with facility. It is widely distributed throughout Europe, except for Ireland and Iceland, and in Scandinavia occurs only in the south-eastern parts. Its range extends eastwards as far as Japan and it is also found in northwest Africa. Individuals from central Europe, generally transient migrants, wend their way in a south-westerly direction during the winter months, whereas populations from western and southern Europe do not leave their nesting grounds all year. The hawfinch builds its nest at the end of April or the beginning of May, generally in broadleaved trees and often in fruit trees, from 2 to 10 metres above the ground. Made of roots, plant stalks and grass, it rests on a thick layer of twigs and is lined with hairs or fine roots. The 4 to 6 eggs are incubated by the hen alone for 14 days, during which time she is fed by the male. The young leave the nest at the age of two weeks. In spring and summer the hawfinch occasionally feeds on insects which it catches on the wing, but the mainstay of its diet is various seeds and kernels. It is fond of visiting cherry orchards, its behaviour there being so quiet and cautious that only the cracking sound as it splits the cherry stones reveals its presence. The young are fed insects at first and later soft seeds.

Length: 16.5 cm. The female is not as richly coloured as the male.
Voice: A sharp 'ptik' or also two-syllable 'ptik-it' or 'tzecip'.
Song: Soft and unobtrusive.
Size of Egg: 19.8—27.6 × 13.1—19.5 mm.

asian Siskin

Fringillidae

duelis spinus

The Eurasian siskin, one of the smallest members of the finch family, makes its home in coniferous, mainly spruce woods, in both lowland country and mountains. It is found in central Europe, Scandinavia, Italy, southern France, Ireland and northern England, its range extending eastwards as far as western Siberia. The siskin is particularly fond of places alongside brooks, in which it loves to bathe. In winter it leaves the woods to form flocks that roam in birch and alder groves, as well as in the vicinity of brooks and streams, where it feeds on birch and alder seeds. Its diet also includes the seeds of thistles. On occasion it nips the buds of evergreens, and will sometimes feed on small berries. It is a very agile forager, clambering swiftly to the tips of branches and often hanging head downwards, similar to the antics of the tit family. Individuals from northern Europe frequently travel en masse to more southerly areas, often as far as the Mediterranean, returning to their breeding grounds at the end of March. The female builds the nest at the tip of a branch, high up in a coniferous tree, generally more than twenty metres above the ground. It is made of slender twigs, bits of bark, lichen and moss and lined with feathers, down and hairs. The 3 to 5 eggs are incubated for 13 days by the hen alone, but she is assisted by the male in feeding the young, primarily with aphids and small caterpillars in the beginning. The young birds leave the nest after two weeks and before long, usually in June, the siskin lays a second clutch.

Length: 12 cm. The female is greyish with grey head.
Voice: Sound resembling 'tsy-zi', in flight often 'tsooeet'.
Song: Pleasant soft chirps and twitters.
Size of Egg: 14.7—18.5 ×11.1—13.6 mm.

Bullfinch

Pyrrhula pyrrhula

During the winter months, especially when there is a great deal of snow, one might come across a great number of brightly coloured birds in rowan woods, at the edges of forests, as well as in parks and gardens. They are bullfinches, which fly to central and southern Europe in vast numbers from their homes in the north. Elsewhere, the bullfinch is distributed throughout most of Europe, except Spain, and in many places is a resident bird. It is found chiefly in coniferous forests with dense undergrowth, both in lowland country and in the mountains, though it often also frequents over-grown parks and large gardens. At the end of April the female begins to build the nest, quite close to the ground, in thick hedges or coniferous trees. The structure is woven of twigs and the hollow is lined with hairs and lichen, sometimes also with fine roots. The male keeps his mate company during this period, both of them being very quiet and unobtrusive and concealing themselves adroitly. The clutch, numbering 5 eggs, is incubated by the hen for 12 to 14 days; only sometimes is she relieved by the male. The young are fed by both parents for 12 to 16 days in the nest, chiefly on insects, and for a short while longer after they have fledged. In June or July they usually have a second brood. Bullfinches feed on seeds and berries and in early spring attack and rip off the buds of flowering trees, especially fruit trees, which makes them extremely unpopular with gardeners.

Length:
14.5—17 cm.
The subspecies of northern Europe is larger.
The female has pinkish-grey underparts.
Voice: A soft, piping sound resembling 'wheeb'.
Song: Composed of piping tones, including 'teek-teek-tioo'.
Size of Egg:
17.0—22.2
× 13.0—15.4 mm.

Common Crossbill

Loxia curvirostra

Fringillidae

The crossbill, so named because of its distinctive bill, the tips of which are crossed, makes its home in coniferous, mostly spruce, forests in mountain areas, occasionally also in lowland country, in central Europe, Scotland, the Pyrenees, the Alps and Scandinavia. It is a resident bird, but frequently appears in places it has not visited for years. Northern populations sometimes invade southern Europe, depending on the abundance of cones, especially spruce and pine, in any particular year. The mainstay of its diet are the seeds of cones, which the crossbill extracts with its beak and which it also feeds to the young. It occasionally eats insects, mostly beetles found on conifers. It breeds mainly from January to April. The nest is built by the female, without any help from the male, though he keeps her company during this period. The 4 eggs are usually incubated by the female for 14 to 15 days, during which time she is fed by the male with food from his crop. The nestlings are born with a straight bill, the tips becoming crossed only after they have reached the age of three weeks. During the first week the family is fed by the male, so that the hen may shelter the young from the cold. After two weeks the young leave the nest and roam the countryside in the company of their parents as they seek food. It was once believed that if a caged brick-red male turned yellow in captivity, he would cure the fever of a sick member of the family. The fact is that the male's coloration often becomes dulled in captivity.

Length: 16.5 cm.
The female's plumage is greenish.
Voice: Sounds resembling 'chip chip chip'.
Song: Chattering, flute-like.
Size of Egg: 19.4—25.5 × 14.1—17.5 mm.

♂

♀

Woodlark

Alaudidae

Lullula arborea

The woodlark, distributed throughout the whole of Europe, except its most northern parts and Ireland, frequents dry, sandy and stony localities with pine trees, shrub-dotted meadows and heaths. It is a migrant, but birds inhabiting western and southern Europe are resident, these areas being also the places where northern populations spend their winter months. The woodlark returns to its breeding grounds in March, but in central Europe this may be as early as the end of February. The birds pair immediately on arrival, if they have not already done so during the return trip from their winter quarters. Shortly after arrival they start building their nest on the ground amidst heather, beneath a young pine tree or in thickets. It is made of roots, plant stalks and moss and lined with hairs and plant fibres. The clutch, numbering 4 to 5 eggs, is incubated by the hen alone for 13 to 15 days. The young are fed by both parents with insects, their larvae and spiders, usually for 13 to 15 days in the nest and a short time after fledging. The woodlark then generally builds a new nest in another spot and lays a second clutch from June or July to August. On leaving the nest the birds form flocks that roam the woods in search of seeds, though they may also be found on fields during the migrating season. The woodlark sings mostly at night or as twilight falls, but its voice may also be heard during the day, from early April until August. Often sought after by bird-catchers in former days, it is now protected by law.

Length: 15 cm.
The male and female have like plumage.
Voice: Characteristic 'toolee' or 'toolooeet'.
Song: Sounds resembling 'lu-lu-lu-lu'.
Size of Egg: 18.0—24.0 × 14.5—17.4 mm.

Tree Pipit
Anthus trivialis

Motacillidae

The tree pipit is widely distributed throughout Europe, except for Spain and Iceland, occurring also in parts of Asia as far as northern Siberia. It is a migratory bird that spends the winter in Africa south of the Sahara, returning in April to its nesting grounds in thin woodlands, open glades or meadows with scattered pine trees, and in woodland margins and forest clearings. It may be seen both in lowland country and the mountains. The birds do not pair until the end of April when the males begin their trilling, which is similar in sound to the canary's song. As he sings the male flies up from his perch at the top of a tree, spreads his wings and tail and descends slowly in a spiral, without pausing in his song until he alights. In May to June the female hatches the 4 to 6 eggs in the nest, usually located in a hollow in a clump of grass or heather. The nest is made of plant stalks, moss and lichens and lined with grass and hairs. The young, hatched after 12 to 13 days, are fed by both parents with insects, mostly mosquitoes and butterflies, various larvae and small spiders. They leave the nest at the age of 10 to 14 days, as yet incapable of flight, and conceal themselves in the immediate vicinity, where the parent birds continue to feed them a further two weeks. When the young have fledged they and the adult birds roam fields in search of leaf beetles, weevils, the caterpillars of turnip and other moths, as well as aphids; thus these birds are among the most beneficial to man.

Length: 15 cm.
Voice: When courting a long drawn-out 'teeze', the alarm note 'sip sip sip'.
Song: Sounds resembling 'chew chew chew chew', followed by long drawn-out 'seea-seea-seea'.
Size of Egg: 18.0—23.5 × 14.7—17.2 mm.

Golden Oriole

Oriolus oriolus

Oriolidae

In late spring, when the nights are already warm, one may hear the melodious, flute-like song of the golden oriole, returned from its winter quarters in far away tropical Africa to its breeding grounds in large parks and deciduous woods. The golden oriole is distributed throughout most of Europe, but is absent in Scandinavia, the British Isles and Iceland. It frequents mainly oak and other broad-leaved woods, more rarely field groves or thin pine woods, and is sometimes found in old parks. At the end of May or the beginning of June the golden oriole weaves its hammock-shaped nest of long thin stalks and grasses, which it suspends between the forks of terminal tree branches, about four metres above the ground. The upper edge of the nest is firmly woven round the boughs on either side. The 3 to 5 eggs are incubated 14 to 15 days by the hen alone, the male relieving her for a brief interval only rarely. The young leave the nest at the age of 14 to 15 days. The golden oriole feeds chiefly on insects and their larvae, sometimes capturing bees and other hymenopterous insects on the wing; spiders and molluscs are also eaten. The diet also includes berries and soft fruits, the birds being fond of visiting orchards where they eat ripe cherries, as well as grapes, red currants and other fruits. In August they set out on the journey to their winter quarters. The golden oriole is a very shy and wary bird which, though often heard, is rarely seen amidst the thick foliage of tall trees.

Length: 24 cm. Female coloured yellow-green.
Song: Flute-like whistling notes that sound like 'weela-weeo' or 'chuck-chuck-weeo'. The male and female also make harsh jay-like croaking calls.
Size of Egg: 27.8—36.0 × 19.9—23.5 mm.

Raven

Corvus corax

Corvidae

During the Middle Ages the raven was a common visitor to the gallows of central Europe. Since then it has completely disappeared in some places, in others it is still plentiful, especially in the Alps, the Carpathians and areas north of Berlin. Its distribution embraces the whole of Europe but is irregular. The raven frequents woodland, cliffs, the tundra in the north and in eastern Europe may even be found on buildings. It is a resident bird but after fledging roams far afield. The nest is often built as early as February by the female from materials which include twigs, moss and hairs, brought by the male. Pairs of birds, remaining together for life, generally use the same nest for years, making only necessary renovations. The 4 to 6 eggs are incubated mostly by the hen, though she is occasionally relieved by the male. The young hatch after 19 to 23 days and remain in the nest 40 to 42 days. The parent birds bring them food in a special throat sac. The raven is an omnivorous bird, but exhibits a preference for meat. It feeds mainly on carrion, but also on smaller animals which it can kill easily with its huge beak. In the vicinity of its nest it will attack even a large predator fearlessly. In the wild it is cautious and vigilant, even after the young have fledged, but if reared in captivity from birth it is quickly tamed.

Length: 63.5 cm.
Wing span:
120 cm. The male and female have like plumage.
Voice: In flight a deep, repeated 'prruk', courting call sounding like 'tok'. It mimics various sounds, including the human voice.
Size of Egg:
42.5—63.0
×29.0—42.5 mm.

Crow

Corvidae

Corvus corone

The crow is widespread throughout the whole of Europe. There are two subspecies: the carrion crow *(Corvus corone corone)*, inhabiting western and southwestern Europe and part of central Europe, and the hooded crow *(Corvus corone cornix)*, inhabiting the remaining territory and found also in Scotland and Ireland. Where their distribution overlaps the two races often interbreed. The crow is a resident bird or a transient migrant, large flocks flying to central and western Europe from north and east in the winter. During the breeding season it frequents open woodlands, field groves and thickly overgrown parks in cities. It builds its nest in March, usually in trees at a height of five metres or more. The structure is made of dry twigs, mud and turf, and lined with moss, grass, hairs, sheep's wool and bits of rags. A new nest takes some 8 to 10 days to build, but crows often use old nests which they renovate as necessary. The female incubates the 4 to 6 eggs herself for 18 to 21 days. During this time the male brings her food, as well as food for the newly hatched nestlings for the first 5 to 7 days. After that both partners share the duties of attending the nestlings. At the age of 28 to 35 days the young leave the nest and roam the countryside with the parent birds. Flocks of crows visit the edges of ponds, lakes and river margins where they find plentiful food remnants. Crows are omnivorous birds. They collect seeds, berries, beech nuts, insects and their larvae, molluscs and carrion, besides which they also hunt fieldmice and other small vertebrates.

Length: 47 cm.
Wing span:
95 to 100 cm.
The male and female have like plumage.
Voice: A deep 'kraa' or croaking 'keerk'.
Song: Composed of like notes and heard in the spring months.
Size of Egg:
33.5—52.7
×26.0—29.7 mm.

2

Jay

Garrulus glandarius

All of Europe, excepting Iceland and northern Scandinavia, provides a home for the jay, which frequents woodlands with undergrowth from lowland to mountain elevations. It is most abundant, however, in woods where oak stands predominate. Mostly a resident bird, it roams the countryside after fledging, but inhabitants of northern Europe sometimes fly in large flocks to central Europe during the winter. The nest is built in spring, from April to May, generally amidst the dense branches of spruce trees on the margins of forests, at a height of four metres or more above the ground. It is usually constructed of dry twigs and a layer of plant stalks and roots, but sometimes is made of moss and lined with grass. The clutch, consisting of 5 to 7 eggs, is incubated by the female for a period of 16 to 17 days. Both parents feed the young until the age of 20 to 21 days when they leave the nest and roam the countryside. Several families will later combine to form a flock. When crossing open territory, however, the flocks break up and the birds fly singly and spaced far apart, converging again only after they have reached a forest. The diet consists of both vegetable and animal food and the jay is likewise fond of birds' eggs. In the autumn flocks visit oak woods, where they collect acorns. The jay is an extremely wary bird and, on sighting a human being, immediately utters a loud cry. In the vicinity of the nest, however, it is very quiet and cautious. The jay can imitate various sounds and birds raised in captivity can be taught to mimic words.

Length: 34 cm.
Wing span:
54 cm. The male
and female have
like plumage.
Voice:
A penetrating
'skraaak' and
sometimes
a mewing note.
Size of Egg:
28.2—36.0
×21.0—25.6 mm.

Black Stork

Ciconia nigra

The black stork inhabits damp coniferous and mixed woods in northeastern, eastern and central Europe as well as in Spain. It prefers lowlands, but may be found also in mountains near ponds, larger brooks, streams and rivers. European populations depart for eastern and southern Africa in August and September, sometimes visiting England en route, and return again at the end of March or in April. The black stork usually starts building its nest in late April or early May. A large, flat structure, it is made of twigs and lined with smaller twigs, moss and grass and located about fifteen metres above the ground on the branches of a tree, usually close to the trunk. Sometimes the black stork uses an abandoned raptor's nest as a foundation for its own and in the mountains will even build it on the ledge of a cliff. The 3 to 5 eggs are incubated by both partners for 30 to 34 days and both bring the nestlings food, in quest of which they fly great distances, often several kilometres from the nest. The young leave the nest after 54 to 63 days. The diet consists mainly of fish, which is caught in streams, ponds and small rivers, but it also feeds on amphibians, small mammals, larger insects and other invertebrates. It also forages in woodland meadows or in the vicinity of riverine forests where it nests. The black stork is a far shyer bird than the closely related white stork. Unlike the latter, it never places its head on its back and does not clap its bill. Hybrids resulting from the crossing of the black and white stork have been bred in captivity.

Length: 96 cm. The male and female have like plumage. The bill and legs of the young are greyish-green.
Voice: Hissing sounds resembling 'feeoo'.
Size of Egg: 60.0—74.3 ×44.0—54.7 mm.

Honey Buzzard

Pernis apivorus

Accipitridae

The honey buzzard is a common inhabitant of all woodlands, especially lowland forests. It is distributed throughout all of Europe, but does not nest in England, Ireland, Iceland and northern and western Scandinavia. A migratory bird, it spends the winter in tropical and southern Africa, journeying from its breeding grounds in August or early September and returning again in April or May. Soon after its arrival in spring it performs its courtship flight above the wood selected as its territory. The large nest of twigs, lined with fresh green twigs and leaves, is built by both partners high in a tree, usually 15 to 22 metres above the ground, though the female performs the greater part of the task. Sometimes the honey buzzard takes over an ·abandoned goshawk's or common buzzard's nest. Even after the young have hatched the adult birds continue to cover the nest with fresh green twigs. The duties of incubating the two eggs are generally shared by the partners for a period of 30 to 35 days; instances have been recorded of the male alone hatching the eggs following the death of the female. As the partners change places on the nest they clap their bills and utter loud cries. The duties of feeding are also shared, the diet during the first few days consisting of wasps and wasp larvae, which the honey buzzard digs out of the ground. The birds feed also on other insects, occasionally on small vertebrates and even soft fruits. The young leave the nest after 35 to 45 days, but return to it at night for a short while longer.

Length: 55 cm.
Wing span: 120 to 126 cm. The male and female have like coloration; often they show marked variation.
Voice: A high-pitched 'kee-er' and also a fast-repeated 'kikiki'.
Size of Egg: 44.9—60.0 ×37.0—44.4 mm.

Sparrow Hawk

Accipiter nisus

Accipitridae

The sparrow hawk — the most common bird of prey — is found throughout Europe. It frequents smaller forests and field groves. When the young have fledged the birds roam the countryside, though many fly southwest at the end of August or September, returning in March or April to their nesting grounds which are selected by the males; the females return somewhat later. The nest of dry twigs, lined with hair, is built in a spruce tree. The sparrow hawk selects another tree nearby to use as its resting place. On the ground below this tree one will find regurgitated undigested food such as bones, hairs, and the like. The 4 to 6 eggs are incubated by the hen for 33 days, but the male brings her food, which she takes from him at a particular spot near to the nest. The female begins incubating as soon as the first, second or third egg is laid. Thus the young hatch successively, the last ones often becoming the victims of the elder and larger nestlings, especially when there is a lack of food. Initially the male hunts for prey, mostly small birds, which he plucks clean at a selected spot before passing it to the female. When the nestlings are a week old the female also forages for food, which she shares out between the young. After the first two weeks, when the young are able to tear their own food, the male brings it to them directly instead of first passing it to the hen. The sparrow hawk hunts prey within a territory measuring some 2 to 5 kilometres in diameter. The young leave the nest at the age of 26 to 31 days.

Length:
28 to 38 cm.
The female is larger.
Wing span:
Male — 60 cm,
female — up to 80 cm.
Voice: Beside the nest a repeated 'leek-leek-leek', when alarmed 'kew kew', also a soft ,keeow'.
Size of Egg:
34.2—46.7
×27.5—36.0 mm.

Goshawk

Accipitridae

Accipiter gentilis

The goshawk makes its home in woods near fields and meadows, in both lowland or mountainous country. It is distributed throughout Europe, but does not nest in England (except very occasionally), Ireland and Iceland. It is a resident bird, remaining in its breeding grounds the year round or roaming the adjacent countryside; inhabitants of northern and eastern Europe, however, often fly to central Europe in winter. The large nest, of sticks and twigs, is built high in the top of a pine or spruce tree from April to May, but the bird's courtship flights may be observed as early as March. The female lays 3 to 4 eggs which she incubates 35 to 38 days, mostly by herself, being relieved only occasionally by the male. She stays with the nestlings for the first ten days, during which time the male supplies food, which the hen divides before passing it to the young, eating the remnants herself. The male is unable to feed the nestlings, and should the hen die during this period they meet the same fate. Later, the hen joins her partner in foraging for food. The young leave the nest after 41 to 43 days and, when fully independent, scatter throughout the countryside, usually settling within 100 kilometres of the home nest. Occasionally young birds from northern Europe have been known to fly as far as 1500 kilometres from where they were born. The goshawk preys mostly on birds, some as large as the heron and, mainly during the winter months, will capture owls such as the long-eared owl and barn owl.

Length:
48 to 58 cm.
The female is larger.
Wing span:
Male — 100 to 105 cm, female — 130 to 140 cm.
The young lack the transverse barred markings.
Voice: A lengthy 'gig-gig-gig', the young utter a piping 'kee'.
Size of Egg:
51.0—65.0
×40.6—51.0 mm.

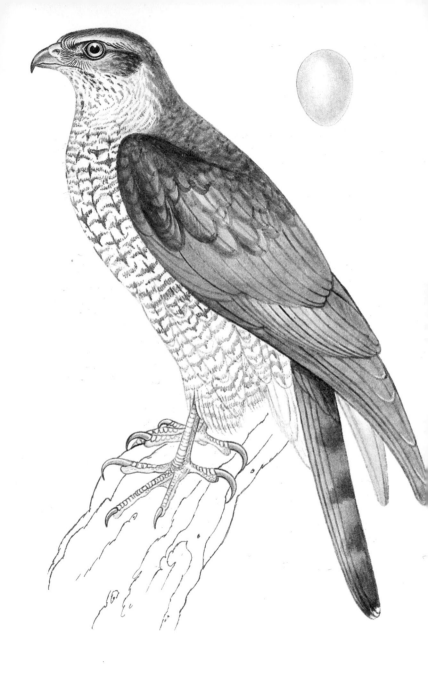

Common Buzzard

Buteo buteo

Accipitridae

At the end of February the common buzzard may be seen circling above a wood, suddenly plummeting to the ground and the next instant soaring up again. This large bird of prey is one of the most common raptors of Europe, where it is absent only in the northernmost regions. It frequents forests of all kinds, from lowland to mountain elevations, preferring locations where woods alternate with fields and meadows. It usually remains in its nesting territory throughout the year, which measures from 3 to 4 kilometres in diameter, or roams the countryside far and wide after fledging. Many inhabitants of northern Europe migrate southwest in winter. In April the buzzard builds its nest high in the treetops, though in England it will also build on cliffs. The structure is made of twigs and lined with leaves, moss and hair; the edge is often decorated with leaves or seaweed and broken twigs may be added to it during the incubation period. Both partners share the duties of sitting on the 2 to 4 eggs for 28 to 49 days, though the female bears the brunt of the task. The nestlings are fed at first by the female, who takes the prey from the male, but later he also feeds them. The young leave the nest after 41 to 49 days, but continue to be fed a further four weeks by the parent birds. The mainstay of the diet are field-mice and other small rodents. It is interesting to note that a buzzard will often wait on the ground outside the hole of a fieldmouse, sometimes without moving for hours, until it succeeds in outwitting its wary prey.

Length: 53 cm.
Wing span:
117 to 137 cm.
There is a marked variation in the colouring.
Voice: A long, plaintive
'pee-oo'.
Size of Egg:
49.8—63.8
×39.1—49.0 mm.

Peregrine Falcon

Falco peregrinus

Often a falcon can be seen circling a church spire, snatching suddenly at one of the hundreds of wild pigeons that are the scourge of modern-day cities. It is because of them that the peregrine falcon, a handsome raptor, is distributed throughout the whole of Europe, for pigeons are the mainstay of its diet, even during the nesting period. The peregrine also hunts other birds. When capturing prey on the wing it climbs above the intended victim, then plummets downward at a speed of up to 280 kilometres an hour, suddenly slowing its flight to attack, striking upward to sink its long talons into the victim's flesh. On occasion the peregrine will also catch a small mammal. Its nest is built in open country in rocky woodland spots which command a wide view, as well as on coastal cliffs and sometimes on tall city towers. The peregrine falcon often avails itself of an abandoned raptor's nest, especially in wooded regions. The thinly-lined structure holds 3 to 4 eggs, which are incubated by the hen, relieved now and then by the male. The nestlings, which emerge after 29 days, are covered with a thick downy coat. For the first few days the male forages for food, which he passes to the hen, who divides it before giving it to the young. The male does not know how to do this and gives food directly to the young only when they are old enough to tear it themselves, usually in the third week after birth. After 35 to 40 days the nestlings leave the nest, but remain within close range for some time.

Length: 43 cm.
Wing span:
Male — 86 to 106 cm, female — 104 to 114 cm.
Voice: A clear and loud, repeated sound resembling 'kek-kek-kek' and a short 'kiack'.
Size of Egg: 46.0—58.9 × 36.3—44.9 mm.

Hobby
Falco subbuteo

The hobby, one of the swiftest of all birds, makes its home in light open woodland, field groves and at the edges of deeper forests throughout most of Europe, but is absent in Ireland, Iceland and northern Scandinavia. It is a migrant and young birds leave for their winter quarters in eastern and southern Africa as early as the middle of August, whereas the older birds do not depart until September or October. At the end of April or beginning of May they return again to their breeding grounds, where they take over the abandoned nests of crows, buzzards and similar birds, making only small alterations. Then follow their breathtaking courtship flights, during which they circle high in the air, then plummet to the ground and immediately sweep up again. The partners generally take turns incubating the three eggs for a period of 28 days. For the first few days after the young are hatched only the male hunts prey, passing it to the female, who waits for it at some distance from the nest. Later she also joins in the search for food. Larger prey, such as a small bird, is passed by the male to the hen, who then feeds it to the nestlings, but insects are fed by the male directly. Both parents are very conscientious in their care of the young, bringing them food every two or three hours; but, when the food source is insects, they are fed several times an hour. At the age of 23 to 34 days the young leave the nest, but continue to be fed by the parent birds for several weeks more.

Length: 33 cm.
Wing span: 75 to 79 cm. The male's tibial feathers are russet, those of the female creamy-white.
Voice: A short 'keu' or 'ket' or lengthy 'kikiki'.
Size of Egg: 36.5—46.5 ×29.6—35.7 mm.

Merlin

Falconidae

Falco columbarius

Northern Europe, England, Ireland and Iceland are the home of the merlin, smallest of European falcons. The inhabitants of northern Europe generally migrate south to spend the winter in the Mediterranean and northern Africa, but some years they remain in central Europe, where they can be seen from the end of September until February. Birds occurring in England are usually resident. April or early May sees them again in their nesting grounds: moorland, tundras, coastal areas or open woodlands, usually conifer forests, but also in empty scrub country. The merlin does not build the nest as a rule, laying its eggs in a depression which may be on the ground or a rock ledge, though occasionally it takes over the abandoned nests of crows or other birds. The 3 to 5 eggs are incubated mostly by the hen for 28 to 32 days, the male generally remaining close by on a high perch, though he sometimes relieves the hen. The young leave the nest at the age of four weeks. The merlin hunts small birds and during the winter in central Europe its diet consists mostly of sparrows, finches, chaffinches and other small common birds. It also captures house martins if they have not already gone south. The diet includes also an abundance of insects and, in dire circumstances, the merlin is known to catch a mouse or other small mammal. It is very agile and can be identified by the conspicuously long, pointed wings, resembling those of the swallow. The merlin was a popular bird in falconry, being trained to hunt small birds.

Length: 28 cm.
Wing span: 61 to 64 cm. The male is bluish-grey, the female russet-grey.
Voice: Resembling that of the kestrel and sounding like 'kikikiki'. The female utters a slow 'eep-eep'.
Size of Egg: 35.0—44.0 ×28.0—33.8 mm.

Capercaillie
Tetrao urogallus

Tetraonidae

Largest of the European grouse, the capercaillie, frequents woodlands, mostly conifer forests with dense undergrowth, in the mountains and hill country. In the north it may also be found in lowland areas. Native to Scotland, the Pyrenees, northern and central Europe, it remains in its breeding grounds throughout the year. Except during the courting season it is a very shy bird and adept at concealing itself. It is only by accident that one may sometimes flush it from cover when walking in the woods. The spring courtship display, however, is conspicuous and remarkable and well known to hunters. During one phase of the display, which takes place while it is still dark, the cock is 'deaf' and 'blind' for a few seconds. When dawn breaks he flies down to the ground, often engaging in battle with a rival. While this takes place the hens sit waiting on nearby branches, and are then led off by the victor. The nest is a hollow in the ground which the hen digs, usually at the base of a tree trunk, and it is lined with grass and leaves. She incubates the 5 to 8 eggs alone for 26 to 29 days, and then rears the young which, able to feed by themselves, she guides in search of food. She also shelters them under her wings and provides them with protection. The chicks are coloured yellow-russet with dark spots, and by the age of 10 days are able to fly about and begin to roost on branches at night. The diet consists chiefly of insects, berries, buds and shoots of conifers. The capercaillie is a popular game bird.

Length:
Male — 94 cm,
female — 67 cm.
Weight:
Male — 5 to 6 kg,
female —2.5
to 3 kg.
Marked sexual
dimorphism.
Voice: The male's
courting call
begins with
a rapidly
accelerating
'tik-up, tik-up,
tik-up', ending
with a 'pop',
followed by
hissing and
whispering; the
hen's call is a
pheasant-like
'kok-kok'.
Size of Egg:
50.8—62.2
×39.0—43.5 mm.

Black Grouse

Lyrurus tetrix

Tetraonidae

The black grouse inhabits northern, eastern and central Europe, nesting also in England. It is most abundant in the arctic tundra, but occurs also in marshland with birch trees, light deciduous and mixed woods, as well as in mountain areas and among peat bogs. It visits also meadows and fields near woods, or forest clearings, where it performs its courtship display in the spring. As many as a hundred cocks will arrive at the courting grounds before sunrise, where they perform all sorts of antics, hopping about, drooping their wings and uttering burbling sounds. It terminates when they leap up and attack one another with their beaks, though only rarely inflicting serious wounds. As dawn breaks the hens arrive on the scene and then fly off with their chosen partners, one cock being accompanied by several hens. From the middle of May till June the hen scrapes a simple hollow in the ground, which she lines with leaves or grass before laying 7 to 12 eggs. These are incubated for 25 to 28 days by the hen, the cock showing no further interest in the fate of his family. When the young hatch, the hen guides them in search of food and also protects them. The chicks, spotted yellow-black, grow very fast and by the end of October are almost the size of adult birds. The diet consists of insects, worms, molluscs, seeds, berries, plant shoots and grass. The black grouse is a game bird, the cocks being shot during the courtship display. The male's lyre-shaped tail is the prized trophy of a fortunate hunter.

Length:
Male — 61.5 cm, female — 42 cm.
Weight:
Male — 1.5 kg, female — up to 1 kg.
Marked sexual dimorphism.
Voice: The male utters a sound resembling 'tchu-shwee' and a whistling sound when he takes to the air, the female's call is a loud 'kok-kok'.
Size of Egg:
46.0—56.3 ×33.4—38.5 mm.

Hazel Hen

Tetraonidae

Tetrastes bonasia

Mixed woods with thickets and groundcover of blueberries and cranberries are the home of the hazel hen. In central Europe its distribution is somewhat local, but in northern Europe, and especially in Scandinavia, it is still plentiful. Its range extends eastward as far as central Asia. The hazel hen does not leave its territory throughout its lifetime, keeping mostly to thickets and occasionally venturing into clearings, but always remaining close to a place of concealment to which it soon withdraws if danger threatens. In May or June the hen prepares the nest in a hollow beside a tree stump, in heather at the base of a tree trunk, in a clump of grass or other well concealed spot, lining it with a thin layer of leaves or dry grass. The 7 to 10 eggs are incubated by the hen alone for a period of 21 to 25 days, hers being also the duty of rearing the young. Soon after the down of the newly-hatched chicks has dried they follow in the wake of the hen, who guides them in search of food, which they can gather for themselves almost from the moment of birth until they are a few days old. When they are able to fly about and perch on branches for the night, the hen still shelters and protects them. At first they feed on insects, their larvae, worms and spiders, but they also eat green shoots and grass. Adults feed on seeds, berries, buds and plant shoots, and in early spring are fond of nibbling catkins. In some countries, especially in central Europe, it has become a rare species and is protected by law.

Length:
Male — 36.5 cm, female — 34 cm. The female lacks the black throat and is not as brightly coloured as the male.
Voice: A whistling sound 'tsissi-tseri-tsi, tsi, tsi, tsiu'.
Size of Egg: 36.1—45.4 ×27.0—30.7 mm.

Common Pheasant

Phasianus colchicus

Phasianidae

The common pheasant was introduced to many parts of Europe in the Middle Ages. It quickly became acclimatized and was soon a common game bird, autumn pheasant shoots remaining popular to this day. Other subspecies from China were later introduced into Europe, where they interbred. The pheasant is generally found in light woods, field groves, thickets beside water, and also in large parks. It is particularly abundant in lowlands, but is common also in hill country. It is a resident bird, remaining in its territory throughout the year. During the spring courting season the cock utters his characteristic harsh note with head held erect, usually following this with a bout of wing fluttering. With a short hopping motion he then circles a chosen hen, or engages in battle with other cocks. After the courting season he pays no further attention to the hen or the young. The hen scrapes a simple hollow in the ground, which she lines with dry leaves or grass, and then lays 8 to 15 eggs which she incubates alone, generally for a period of 24 to 25 days. The chicks begin to fly at the age of two weeks and roost in the treetops with the hen. The diet consists of various seeds, berries, green plant shoots, insects, worms and molluscs. In winter it is necessary to put out food for pheasants wherever they occur in greater numbers. Many countries have established large pheasant preserves, where the birds are given partial freedom or kept in aviaries.

Length:
Male — 79 cm,
female — 60 cm.
Marked sexual
dimorphism.
Voice: The male's
courting call is
a harsh 'korrk-
kok'.
Size of Egg:
39.0—51.1
×32.4—37.6 mm.

Woodcock
Scolopax rusticola

Scolopacidae

The woodcock is established throughout Europe, excepting for the most northern regions. Inhabitants of western and southwestern Europe stay for the winter, those from other areas travel to countries bordering the Mediterranean — Spain and France being the chief winter haven of these birds. From the middle of March to April the woodcock returns to its breeding grounds in lowland woods, mostly deciduous or mixed forests. The birds pair following a courtship display, in which the hen sits on the ground and entices the male by spreading her tail, which has a conspicuous white patch, and at the same time uttering a special cry. As soon as he sees or hears her, the male descends rapidly to the ground and hops around the hen in a sort of dance. Sometimes two males arrive at the same time, and soon become involved in combat. In April, and often for a second time in June, the female lays 4 eggs in a shallow scrape in the ground, lined with a few leaves and moss. The young hatch after 20 to 23 days, and as soon as their down has dried leave the nest, remaining close to the hen. The woodcock gathers its food (insects, their larvae, molluscs and worms) on the ground, often probing among soft soil and leaves with its long beak, which is provided with special sensory cells to signal the presence of its prey. The woodcock is hunted at twilight, and though it is not an important game bird its meat is considered a great delicacy.

Length: 34 cm. The male and female have like plumage. The young are striped reddish-brown.
Weight: Circa 300 grams.
Voice: During the courting season the male utters a soft croaking 'orrrt-orrrt' and a sneeze-like 'tsiwick'.
Size of Egg: 40.1—49.0 ×31.6—36.4 mm.

Wood Pigeon or Ring Dove

Columba palumbus

Columbidae

By the middle of March, flocks of wood pigeons return from their winter quarters in the Mediterranean to their nesting grounds throughout most of Europe. Those which inhabit warmer parts of the Continent are either resident or transient migrants. The wood pigeon is found in all types of woodland, overgrown parks or in large gardens with thick ground cover. Early in spring one may hear the unusual 'clapping' of the males' wings, this being part of their courtship antics. The nest is a flimsy structure of twigs, haphazardly laid on top of each other, and is generally located on the branch of a conifer, rarely a deciduous tree, at its junction with the trunk, some 3 to 4 metres above the ground or higher. The male and female take turns incubating the two eggs for 17 to 18 days, and both feed the young with 'pigeon's milk', regurgitated from the crop. The young birds leave the nest at the age of 20 to 29 days, perching on nearby branches, where they continue to be fed by the parents. They are usually about 35 days old before they are capable of independent flight. The adult birds usually have a second brood in June to August, occasionally a third. The diet consists chiefly of seeds, green plant parts and, on occasion, even small invertebrates such as earthworms and molluscs. During the day flocks of wood pigeons may be seen on fields, where they often fall prey to the peregrine falcon. In September and October they again leave their nesting grounds. The wood pigeon is a popular game bird and its meat is tasty.

Length: 40.5 cm. The male and female have like plumage.
Weight: Up to circa 500 grams.
Voice: A cooing note that sounds like 'cooo-coo, coo-coo, coo'.
Size of Egg: 36.5—47.8 ×25.0—33.0 mm.

Stock Dove

Columbidae

Columba oenas

Deciduous and mixed woods, occasionally thin conifer forests and old parks, are places where the stock dove makes its home. This bird, widespread throughout Europe except for the most northern areas, is resident in the west and south. Inhabitants of other regions migrate to southwestern Europe and the Mediterranean in September—October. They return to their breeding grounds as early as the end of February, seeking out locations with old trees which provide cavities for nesting. They sometimes take over an abandoned black woodpecker's hole, will lay their eggs in a man-made nesting box, and are known also to nest in holes in sandbanks. The nest is generally located at least 10 metres above the ground. The stock dove has disappeared from many forests where it was once plentiful because of the lack of suitable nesting cavities. The hollow is lined with dry sticks and small twigs, but some females will lay their clutch of two eggs without bothering to line the cavity. Incubation, shared by both partners, occupies a period of 16 to 17 days, and both feed the young 'pigeon's milk' regurgitated from the crop. At the age of three weeks the young leave the nest, but continue to be fed half-digested seeds and grain by the parents for a short while longer. When their offspring are fully mature, the adult birds often have a second brood. The diet of the mature birds consists mostly of various seeds, but includes small fruits, berries and green plant parts.

Length: 33 cm. The male and female have like plumage.
Weight: Circa 280 grams.
Voice: A cooing note that sounds like 'ooo-roo-oo'.
Size of Egg: 33.0—43.0 ×26.0—31.0 mm.

Turtle Dove

Streptopelia turtur

Columbidae

The purring call of the turtle dove may be heard on a warm April or May day, announcing its return from winter quarters in far-off tropical Africa. This species is plentiful throughout all of Europe, except Scandinavia, and is found also in northwest Africa and western Asia. The turtle dove frequents thin mixed woods with under-growth, field groves, thickets alongside rivers, streams and ponds, as well as parks with thick growths. During the courtship flight the male soars into the air, before gliding down with tail feathers spread wide. The nest, a simple structure of dry sticks and twigs arranged haphazardly on top of each other, is built by both partners, generally 1 to 5 metres above the ground, in bushes and treetops. The two eggs are incubated 14 to 16 days by both parents and both feed the young with 'pigeon's milk', regurgitated from the crop during the first few days. Later the diet consists of various half-digested seeds and grain. The young leave the nest at the age of 14 to 16 days but continue to be fed by the parent birds a short while longer. When the first brood is fully mature, the adult birds have a second, usually in June or July. The turtle dove leaves the woods to visit fields in search of food, and in late summer they gather in small groups in the fields before leaving for the south. The turtle dove is considered a game bird in many countries, but is of little importance to hunters. Agile and swift in flight, it is adept at darting between branches in the treetops, and often eludes an attacking falcon.

Length: 27 cm. The male and female have like plumage.
Voice: A long-drawn-out 'roor-r-r'.
Size of Egg: 27.0—34.6 ×20.0—24.6 mm. The eggs are pure white.

Tawny Owl

Strix aluco

Strigidae

The tawny owl is one of the most common owls in Europe, and remains in its breeding grounds even during severe winters. A denizen of woods, it is found also in parks with old trees and sometimes in a large garden. In mild winters it often nests as early as February, otherwise usually in April. Even before this one can hear it hooting, and the odd sounds caused by the slapping of the wing quills against each other. The nest is usually located in a tree cavity, though the tawny owl will also occupy a large man-made nesting box. Occasionally it will take over an abandoned raptor's nest and has also been known to make its nest in a hollow in the ground, though this is exceptional. The female incubates the 3 to 5 eggs for 28 to 30 days by herself, the male bringing her food during this period and occasionally relieving her on the nest. Since the hen begins incubating as soon as the first eggs are laid, the young hatch successively. For about 10 days after the first nestlings have hatched the hen does not leave the nest. The male supplies the whole family with food, mainly small mammals, but also other vertebrates such as bats, reptiles, amphibians as well as insects. Later the hen assists in hunting, but keeps an eye on the nest during the daytime. Sometimes she feeds the young in the daylight hours, supplying them from stores gathered during the night. At the age of 28 to 36 days the young leave the nest, remaining in its vicinity and continuing to be fed by the parents. When they are 50 days old they launch out on their first flight.

Length: 38 cm.
Wing span: 92 to 94 cm. The male and female have like plumage, which shows marked variation in coloration.
Voice: During the courting season 'hoo-hoo-hoo, oo-oo-oo-oo', sometimes also 'ke-wick'.
Size of Egg: 43.0—51.7 ×34.4—43.3 mm. The eggs are pure white.

Ural Owl

Strix uralensis

Strigidae

The large Ural owl inhabits the deep forests of eastern Scandinavia, northeastern and central Europe, at both lowland and mountain elevations. It is more plentiful in areas where there is an abundance of rodents, for fieldmice and mice are the mainstay of its diet. In the north it feeds mainly on lemmings, but will capture also smaller birds or insects. When there are few rodents in an area the owl population will fall for some years, the majority leaving for regions where food is more plentiful. Apart from this kind of movement, the Ural owl is a resident species. The nest is located in tree cavities, although it will also take over large nests abandoned by raptors. The nest is located at least 4 metres above the ground, but generally at a height of 10 to 20 metres. When there is an insufficient food supply in the given territory, a pair of owls will often not nest at all. As a rule the hen lays 3 to 4 eggs in April, incubating them herself for 27 to 29 days while the male brings her food. He also supplies the food for the young, but they are fed only by the hen. They leave the nest for the first time at the age of 34 days, but often return to it for the night. The Ural owl is a courageous bird that will chase large raptors, and is also known to have attacked humans that have approached too close to its nest. During the winter months, when food in the woods is scarce, it moves from the shelter of the forest to the vicinity of human habitations where it occasionally takes domestic fowl.

Length: Circa 60 cm.
Wing span: 105 to 116 cm. The male and female have like plumage.
Voice: Resembling that of the tawny owl but pitched higher and with a hollower sound, also a deep 'wow-wow-wow' or 'kawveck'.
Size of Egg: 47.1—54.7 ×39.0—44.0 mm. The eggs are pure white.

Pygmy Owl
Glaucidium passerinum

The pygmy owl, smallest of European owls, inhabits conifer forests in lowland and mountain areas throughout Scandinavia, central and north-eastern Europe, and eastward as far as the Amur. Inhabitants of central Europe are resident, those of northern regions are transient migrants. In central Europe it occurs chiefly in moutain areas, such as the Black Forest, Bohemian Forest and the Alps, but it may also be found in deep woods at lower elevations. In some places the pygmy owl is fairly common, but escapes notice in the dense forests where it makes its home. The male's call and the female's lower pitched answering call may be heard as early as December. In April or May the pygmy owl seeks a place to nest, usually in a tree cavity and preferably one made by woodpeckers, but it will also occupy a man-made starling's nesting box hung up in its woodland territory. The clutch generally consists of 4 to 6 eggs and the task of incubating for a period of 28 days falls to the hen alone. The young are fed insects and small birds or mammals. The pygmy owl often stores part of its catch for future use, so the cavity may contain several dozen mice, shrews, sparrows, buntings and other small birds. It hunts its prey both night and day and is very agile. It lies in wait for its victims, perched on a branch, and as soon as it sees a suitable bird will dart out, often catching it on the wing. As a rule it does not hunt in open spaces, keeping to the cover of trees and thickets even when attacking.

Length: 16.5 cm.
Weight: A mere 75 grams. The male and female have like plumage.
Voice: A whistling note that sounds like 'keeoo', 'kitchick' or a bullfinch-like 'whee-whee-whee'.
Size of Egg: 27.0—31.5 ×21.5—24.5 mm.

Eurasian Eagle Owl

Bubo bubo

Strigidae

The Eurasian eagle owl, largest of the European owls, is widespread throughout Europe except for the western parts. It is quite plentiful in some areas, its numbers having increased in recent years, thanks to rigid protection laws. The Eurasian eagle owl makes its home in open woodlands, rocky locations as well as scrub country. It is a resident bird or transient migrant and may be found in both lowland and mountain regions. It nests on cliff ledges, the walls of old castle ruins or simply on the ground; in northern regions it often uses a tree cavity at ground level. The simple nest, sometimes lined with only a few hairs and feathers from the owl's victims, contains 2 to 4 eggs incubated by the female for 32 to 37 days. During this time the male brings her food, which she takes from him at a short distance from the nest. The newly hatched nestlings are cared for by the hen, who also shelters them from both rain and sun. At the age of one to two months, the young leave the nest and perch in its vicinity. By the time they are three months old they can fly well. The eagle owl occupies a large territory, extending as far as 15 kilometres from the nest. It preys on vertebrates as big as a hare or a small fox, but will feed also on insects. The eagle owl is hated by predators and crows, a fact of which hunters took advantage by using it as a decoy. This method of hunting is now forbidden in many countries with the object of protecting birds of prey.

Length: 67 cm.
Wing span:
160 to 166 cm.
The male and female have like plumage.
Voice:
A penetrating note carrying a great distance, sounding like 'ooo-hu', sometimes followed by a guttural chuckle.
Size of Egg:
51.2—73.0 ×42.0—53.7 mm.

Long-eared Owl

Asio otus

Strigidae

The long-eared owl is common throughout Europe except for the most northern parts. It occurs chiefly in small conifer and mixed woods, as well as in field groves, large parks and overgrown gardens. It is faithful to its breeding grounds but many birds, especially inhabitants of northerly regions, sometimes form groups that travel southwest in winter, staying in places where field mice are plentiful, these being the mainstay of the long-eared owl's diet. At the end of March or in April it lays its eggs in the abandoned nests of crows, raptors, jays or the dreys of squirrels, adding only slight variations of its own. The hen incubates the 4 to 6 eggs herself for 27 to 28 days, beginning as soon as the first is laid, and so the young hatch successively. The male brings food for his partner and also the nestlings, but these are fed only by the hen. The male often stands beside the nest and claps his wings against his body with a sharp crack, thus revealing its location. The long-eared owl hunts only after dusk, concealing itself in the thick branches of spruce, pine and other trees during the daytime. Pressed motionless against a branch it often looks like a broken stump, escaping detection by all except an experienced ornithologist. Besides rodents, the long-eared owl hunts small birds and, when the young are being fed, it also captures countless insects, including such harmful pests as chafers. The young leave the nest at the age of 21 to 26 days and perch on neighbouring branches.

Length: 34 cm.
Wing span: 85 to 90 cm. The male and female have like plumage.
Voice: During the courting season a penetrating 'oo-oo-oo', also semi-whistling sounds.
Size of Egg: 35.0—44.7 ×28.0—34.5 mm. The eggs are pure white.

Common Cuckoo

Cuculus canorus

Cuculidae

As early as the middle of April one may hear the familiar melodious call of the male cuckoo, returned to his breeding grounds from far-off tropical or southern Africa. The females, who arrive a week or ten days later, do not make this characteristic call, but a sound resembling that of the woodpecker. Cuckoos often return to the same breeding grounds for several years in succession, and may be found in woods, field groves, large parks, overgrown graveyards as well as thickets beside water or even in large reed beds. The female roams her territory seeking small songbirds' nests and, when she finds one that is suitable, removes any eggs it might contain, depositing her own in their stead, usually similar in colouring to those of the host. From May to July one hen lays about 15 to 20 eggs, each in a different nest. An individual cuckoo lays eggs of like coloration, but often markedly different from those of other cuckoos. The period of incubation is 12 days and, on hatching, the young cuckoo soon tumbles all the eggs and even the rightful progeny of its foster parents out of the nest. The newly hatched cuckoo is completely naked and has very sensitive sensory cells on its back that, during the first four days, react to contact with any foreign object in the nest, including both eggs and the hatched offspring of the foster parents. Adult cuckoos feed on hairy caterpillars. In late July or early September the cuckoo leaves the breeding areas for its winter quarters.

Length: 33 cm. The male and female have like plumage.
Voice: The male's call sounds like 'cuc-coo', the female's like 'kwickkwick-kwick'; the cry of the young resembles 'tseetseetsee'.
Size of Egg: 19.7—26.4 ×14.7—18.8 mm. The eggs show marked variation in colouring.

European Nightjar

Caprimulgus europaeus

The European nightjar returns from its winter haven in eastern and southern Africa in late April or in May. It is widespread throughout Europe, where it frequents light and dry conifer or mixed woods, mainly where in fact there are plenty of pine trees, but it also favours the margins of forests and forest clearings. During the courting period it performs acrobatic feats, clapping its wings simultaneously. During the day it perches lengthwise on a tree branch, its colouring making it practically invisible. When startled it opens its bill wide and spreads its wings and tail in an attempt to frighten off any intruder. When disturbed on the nest it frequently flies up, hovering in the air with wide-open beak in an attempt to ward off the assailant and prevent its approach to the nest. The female lays 2 eggs on the bare ground at the end of May or in June, and both partners take turns at incubating for 16 to 18 days. The young, which leave their 'nest' at the age of 16 to 19 days, are fed insects for a full month. These include chafers and other beetles, as well as moths, including the swift sphinx-moth, which the adult birds catch on the wing after dusk. The nightjar leaves for its winter quarters in August or September. Outside the nesting season it is not shy and often visists pastures, flying close to humans and animals in its pursuit of airborne insects. This accounts for the belief that it visits grazing she-goats and sucks their udders, giving rise to the names by which it is known in many countries as, for example, the German *Ziegenmelker* (nanny-milker).

Length: 27 cm. The female lacks the white patch on the primaries. *Voice:* Flight call is a soft 'goo-ek', alarm call a high 'quick-quick-quick' and the night song a loud, rapid churring, rising and falling, which can last for as long as five minutes. *Size of Egg:* 27.0—36.5 ×20.0—24.0 mm.

European Roller

Coracias garrulus

The roller, a most attractively coloured bird, may be seen in open locations with old trees, in light deciduous woods, or in rows of trees alongside rivers. It inhabits southern and eastern Europe as well as the eastern half of central Europe. It is a common species in the more southerly areas and when migrating may make its way as far as Norway, Finland and Iceland. The winter is spent mainly in eastern Africa, from where it returns at the beginning of May to its favourite breeding locations, lowlands dotted with woods and meadows. It is fond of perching on telegraph and telephone wires or poles, from where it has a good view of the surrounding countryside. The male performs his courtship flight above the tree in which he has located the nest, turning somersaults, darting up, turning on his side and plummeting down again. The female lays 4 to 5 eggs in the nesting cavity, incubating them herself for 18 to 20 days, though occasionally the male relieves her in this task. The hen begins incubating as soon as the first egg is laid. The young leave the nest at the age of 26 to 28 days, but continue to be fed by the parents for a short while after. The food consists of insects, which also form the major part of the adults' diet. The roller is swift and agile, generally catching its prey on the wing. Sometimes it will even capture a small lizard or mouse, beating such a large catch against the ground in order to kill it. In autumn it also nibbles soft fruits. In August or the beginning of September it departs on its southward journey.

Length: 30.5 cm. The male and female have like plumage.
Voice: A loud crow-like 'kr-r-r-r-ak' or 'krak-ak' and a harsh chatter.
Size of Egg: 32.0—40.0 ×25.5—31.5 mm.

Green Woodpecker
Picus viridis

The whole of Europe, except northern Scandinavia, Ireland, Scotland and Iceland, is home to the green woodpecker. It is a resident species, but in winter is also a transient migrant. It frequents light deciduous woods, field groves as well as parks, large gardens, orchards and overgrown grave-yards. During the courting period in spring the male and female pursue each other in the air or round the trunk of a tree, uttering loud cries. At the end of April the pair of birds drill a hole in the trunk of a deciduous tree, usually where the wood is soft or has rotted, each taking turns at the task. The pear-shaped cavity, about 50 centi-metres deep, is completed in about two weeks. In addition to the nesting cavity, the green wood-pecker also drills another which serves as sleeping quarters, and both are often used for several years in succession. Sometimes the green woodpecker will nest in a hole in a wall, especially in city parks. The female lays 5 to 7 eggs, which she and the male take turns incubating for 15 to 17 days. The young are born naked and blind and the parents feed them mostly on ants and their pupae. The diet consists also of the larvae of beetles which the woodpecker finds when 'boring' holes in anthills on the ground. In winter the green wood-pecker often drills deep tunnels in the ground to reach hibernating ants in their anthills. Some-times it will visit beehives, breaking the wooden parts in its effort to get at the bees. In winter the woodpecker will often feed from a garden tray.

Length: 32 cm. The female lacks the crimson patch below the eye.
Voice: During the courtship period a very loud ringing 'laugh', the female's note is shorter and does not have the same ring.
Size of Egg: 28.0—33.9 ×20.3—24.0 mm.

Great Spotted Woodpecker

Dendrocopos major

Picidae

All of Europe, except Ireland and the most northern areas, provides a home for one of the most abundant of woodpeckers — the great spotted. It stays for the winter in most areas, though it is also a transient migrant out of the breeding season, but inhabitants of northern Europe sometimes journey south in large flocks. Why they undertake such a long trip is as yet not understood. The great spotted woodpecker occurs in woodlands of all types, in the mountains up to the tree line, but is also found in large numbers in parks and large gardens, orchards and tree avenues. In the winter it often roams the countryside in the company of nuthatches and tits, and will visit a garden feeding tray to nibble sunflower seeds or suet. In spring both partners, though mainly the male, drill a hole about 30 centimetres deep in the trunk of a deciduous or coniferous tree, often using the same cavity for several years. The female lays 5 to 6 eggs, which she and the male take turns incubating for 12 to 13 days. The parents feed the young from the beak, and consequently must bring food to the nest much more often than the green or black woodpecker. At first they make about 40 trips a day, but when the young are some 10 days old the daily trips can total 150 or more. For this reason, the prey must be hunted in the immediate neighbourhood of the nest. The diet consists mainly of insects and their larvae. At the age of 21 to 23 days the young abandon the cavity but remain in the vicinity of the nest. Adult birds also feed on various seeds and grain.

Length: 23 cm. The male has a red patch on the nape.
Voice: A loud 'kik' or 'chick'. In spring it drums with its beak on the trunks or branches of trees.
Size of Egg: 20.0—29.5 × 15.4—21.8 mm.

Black Woodpecker

Picidae

Dryocopus martius

Early in spring, often as early as March, woodlands with old pine trees or beeches echo to the loud drumming sound of the black woodpecker, perched on the stump of a branch which he strikes repeatedly with his beak as he courts a partner. In the middle of April both partners drill a nesting cavity in a tree trunk, which is usually 35 to 55 centimetres deep, though sometimes it can be as much as one metre, depending on the hardness of the wood. The black woodpecker usually selects the trunk of a pine or beech, the task taking some 10 to 15 days with the male doing most of the work. The litter of large woodchips at the base of the tree reveals the presence of its home, and the black woodpecker also excavates cavities in other trees in the vicinity, which he uses as sleeping quarters, all having an oval entrance hole. The 4 to 5 eggs are incubated by both partners for 12 to 13 days, the male sitting on them mainly at night. The young, which remain in the cavity for 23 to 28 days, are fed by both parents, primarily on ants and their pupae. They are fed only a few times each day, but in large quantities. Adult birds feed on the larvae of weevils and bark beetles. When the young have fledged the parents remain in the neighbourhood, whereas their offspring wander as far as several hundred kilometres from the nest. The black woodpecker is widespread in central, northern and eastern Europe and may be found in both mountain areas and lowland country.

Length: 45 cm. The male has a red patch on the forehead.
Voice: A long drawn-out 'kleea', a high, grating 'krri-krri-krri', and a ringing 'choc-choc-choc' flight song.
Size of Egg: 31.0—37.7 × 22.0—27.0 mm.

Ring Ouzel

Turdus torquatus

The mountain areas on the west coast of Scandinavia, England, Ireland, the Alps, Pyrenees and Carpathians are the home of the ring ouzel. It frequents light woods at the dwarf-pine line, but in northern Europe and England it is to be found in moors and rocky places with thickets. Its favourite haunts, however, are mountain slopes sparsely dotted with dwarf-pine and short spruce trees, where it is most often found in the vicinity of rapid flowing mountain streams. In more southerly parts of Europe it is a resident species, but inhabitants of the northern areas fly to countries bordering the Mediterranean in September—November, returning again in mid-March to April. The somewhat untidy nest of twigs, plant stalks and grasses is built low down in trees, often amidst dwarf-pine; occasionally they nest on the ground between stones, adjacent to a mountain stream. The structure is usually well concealed by lichen gathered in the immediate vicinity and added to the other building materials. The 4 to 5 eggs are incubated for 14 days, mostly by the hen, though sometimes the male takes a turn. Both, however, feed the nestlings for 15 to 16 days. On leaving the nest the young conceal themselves in the neighbourhood, usually between stones, and the parents continue to feed them for a further two weeks or so. When their offspring are fully independent the parent birds often build a new nest and rear a second brood. The ring ouzel feeds chiefly on insects and their larvae, small molluscs and worms, and also on berries and soft fruits in the autumn.

Length: 24 cm. Sexual dimorphism.
Voice: A clear, piping 'pee-u' and a blackbird-like 'tac-tac-tac'.
Song: Includes 'tcheru', 'tchivi', 'ti-cho-o' and chuckling.
Size of Egg: 28.9—34.0 ×20.3—24.0 mm.

Rock Thrush

Monticola saxatilis

Turdidae

Southern Europe and the warmest parts of central Europe are the home of the rock thrush. It is found on sunwarmed and dry rocky slopes, in mountains, also in vineyards, old castle ruins and abandoned quarries; it has been known to become established in quarries where work was in progress without appearing to be bothered by the noise and activity. Oddly enough, it is a very shy and wary bird and only rarely seen. As soon as it spots a human being it disappears immediately, and when flying across open spaces it keeps close to thickets or the edge of a wood. The rock thrush returns from its winter quarters in tropical Africa or southwestern Arabia at the end of April and builds a nest of roots, plant stalks and moss, lined with moss and hair, which, to justify its name, it builds in cracks and rock crevices. The 4 to 5 eggs are incubated by the hen alone for a period of 14 to 15 days, the young leaving the nest at the age of two weeks. The rock thrush feeds mainly on insects and their larvae; it also catches butterflies and flies on the wing, and sometimes gathers worms, centipedes, spiders and small molluscs. It leaves the breeding grounds for its winter quarters during the month of September. In former times this bird, especially the male, was prized by bird fanciers for its lovely song and was often kept in cages. In central Europe, where this species is comparatively rare, it is protected by law. If well cared for and fed on insects it lives to a ripe age in the confines of a large cage.

Length: 19 cm. The female is spotted brown and the young have a like coloration.
Voice: Courting note — 'chack chack'.
Song: Flute-like notes and combinations of various melodies learned from other birds.
Size of Egg: 23.2—30.0 ×16.9—21.0 mm.

♀

♂

Redpoll

Acanthis flammea

Fringillidae

The redpoll is primarily a bird of the arctic tundra, from where it invades central and southern Europe in large numbers every autumn. It is found also in alpine regions at the dwarf-pine limits, especially the Swiss and Italian Alps, as well as in England and Ireland, where it is found even in lowland country, and more recently in many places in central Europe. It is becoming more and more plentiful in central Europe, where it nests in mountains and hill country. Its characteristic habitat is pure birch stands or mixed woods with birch. In May it builds a nest of slender twigs, stalks and grasses, lined with hairs and horsehair, usually located in bushes in the mountains, in dwarf-pine or short trees, generally 1.5 to 3 metres above the ground. In the arctic regions it usually does not nest until June. Frequently several pairs join to form a large nesting colony. The 5 to 6 eggs are incubated for 10 to 12 days by the hen, while the male brings her food. The young, which leave the nest at the age of 10 to 14 days, are fed insects and insect larvae by both parents, who continue to feed them for a further 10 to 14 days after they have fledged. The mainstay of the adult birds' diet is seeds, especially those of alder, birch and conifers. When the offspring are sufficiently independent, the parent birds often rear a second brood. In winter, groups of redpolls often visit parks and gardens which have birch or other trees and seed-bearing bushes.

Length: 12.5 cm. The male has a redder throat and rump.
Voice: The characteristic flight call is a rapid 'chuch-uch-uch' or 'tiu-tiu-tiu'. Alarm note is a plaintive 'tsooeet'.
Song: A sustained series of brief trills.
Size of Egg: 14.3—17.5 ×10.0—13.2 mm.

Water Pipit

Anthus spinoletta

Motacillidae

The water pipit inhabits barren rocky locations with screes in high mountains above the tree line. It prefers large spaces with a great many scattered boulders and clumps of grass. Its range includes southern and southeastern Europe, as well as parts of central Europe (the Alps and Carpathians), England and the coast of Scandinavia. Northern populations migrate south to central Europe in winter, where the species is faithful to its breeding grounds, though some inhabitants of central Europe travel farther south as proved by ringed birds. Water pipits nesting in high mountains descend to lower altitudes during the winter, forming small groups that roam the countryside in the vicinity of water or marshes. In April they return to their breeding territories and, in May or June, build their nests among clumps of grass, under an overhanging bush or stone. The construction is of fine plant stalks, lichen and moss which is lined with fine hairs. The walls of the nest are unusually thick — as much as 5 centimetres. The female lays 4 to 6 eggs, which she incubates herself for 14 to 16 days. The young, which leave the nest at the age of two weeks, are fed by both parents with insects and their larvae, as well as spiders and worms. After fledging, the whole family roams the countryside, often keeping close to human habitations. The water pipit is an active bird that continually runs about on the ground, flits here and there, hops up on a rock, looks about and then resumes its search for food.

Length: 16 cm. The male and female have like plumage.
Voice: Courting note that sounds like 'tseep-eep'.
Song: In flight, comprises notes resembling 'tsip' and 'jeep'.
Size of Egg: 18.9—24.0 ×14.0—16.5 mm.

Chough

Pyrrhocorax pyrrhocorax

Corvidae

Britain, France, Switzerland, Italy, Sicily, Spain and the Alps are the home of the chough. This bird with its brightly coloured bill may be seen in large numbers on coastal cliffs or high in the mountains, generally at elevations of about 1500 metres, but even at more than 3500 metres above sea level. It is faithful to its breeding grounds, remaining there even in winter, but descending into the valleys when the cold weather sets in. Choughs congregate in groups and are also colonial nesters, a single colony comprising 40 to 60 pairs of birds. The nest of twigs, roots, dry grass, wool and hair is built at the end of April or in May in rock cavities or crevices, sometimes on a church steeple, castle ruins or the roofs of tall buildings. The female usually lays 3 to 6 eggs, and these may show marked variation in coloration. The period of incubation is 17 to 21 days, the task falling solely to the hen. The young are fed insects and their larvae by both parents, who make only seven trips a day between 8 in the morning and 3 in the afternoon. Adult birds occasionally capture small vertebrates, and in winter will feed on seeds if a more normal diet is scarce. The young leave the nest at the age of 32 to 38 days, but remain in the company of their parents. They can be distinguished from the adult birds by their orange beaks. On fledging the chough shows little fear of man and groups often visit mountain chalets where they are fed by the guests. Groups of choughs regularly visit water to drink.

Length: 38 cm. The male and female have like plumage.
Voice: A jackdaw-like 'kyaw', a characteristic 'tchuff' and a gull-like 'kwuk-uk-uk' call.
Size of Egg: 34.3—42.0 ×21.5—29.5 mm.

Nutcracker

Nucifraga caryocatactes

The nutcracker inhabits conifer forests in the mountain areas of southern Scandinavia, central and southeastern Europe; its original habitat is the arctic taiga. It is a resident species, but also a transient migrant; some years' populations from as far away as Siberia invade Europe during the winter. The nutcracker generally nests at elevations above 300 metres, but in the Alps it may be found at anything between 800 and 2000 metres above sea level. In northern Europe it is found also in the lowlands. The deep nest is built at the end of February or the beginning of March, among thick branches of spruce trees, generally between 4 and 15 metres above the ground. The structure comprises a foundation of broken twigs on top of which is a layer of moss, lichens and rotting wood, and the hollow is lined with soft grass, leaves and feathers. The 3 to 4 eggs are incubated by the hen alone for 17 to 19 days, during which time she is fed by the male. The young leave the nest at the age of 23 days and, in the company of their parents, roam woods where there is an abundant crop of nuts, beechnuts and other seeds. Frequently they store them in a cache in a tree stump or at the base of a tree trunk and, surprisingly, are able to find these caches again in times of need. Sometimes the birds visit orchards where they pick the seeds from ripe pears, and will also eat insects. They have been known to take the young of songbirds from the nest, although such behaviour is rare.

Length: 32 cm.
Wing span: 59 cm.
The male and female have like plumage.
Voice: Cry like that of the jay; call in spring sounds like 'kror'.
Size of Egg: 30.3—37.5 ×21.5—26.0 mm.

Red-legged Partridge

Alectoris rufa

Phasianidae

The red-legged partridge inhabits the mountain areas, but also lowlands and hills with fields and vineyards, of southwestern Europe and England. In recent years it has been introduced into many parts of central Europe, but without much success to date, for it has many enemies in these new locations, a typical example being the fox. The red-legged partridge prefers stony places covered with grass and sparsely dotted with shrubs, beneath which it builds its nest in a depression in the ground, only sparingly lined with leaves and grass stems. The 8 to 15 eggs are incubated by the hen for 24 days, while the male roams the neighbourhood, returning to his family when the young are born. The nestlings usually leave the hollow on the second day, following in the hen's wake, and by the end of a week begin their first attempts at flight. The parent birds guide them in search of food, which the chicks gather for themselves. Even after they are fully grown the young remain in the company of their parents, families later forming groups of about 20 birds. After sunset they seek shelter in rock crevices or protected rocky ledges, but despite such precautions many red-legged partridges fall prey to raptors and predators. In spring the male's loud cry may be heard before dawn. In winter, flocks of these partridges descend into the valleys to seek places free from snow. Their diet consists of seeds, berries, grass, insects, molluscs and worms. It has been determined that the red-legged partridge eats about 90 different species of plants.

Length: 35 cm. The male and female have like coloration.
Weight: 370 to 770 grams; game bird.
Voice: A 'chuck, chuck-er' call note, explosive 'pitchi-i' alarm signal; also a variable 'tschreck'.
Size of Egg: 41.4 × 31.0 mm on the average.

Ptarmigan
Lagopus mutus

The ptarmigan inhabits the Alps, Scotland, Iceland and northern Europe. In the mountains it occurs at elevations up to the snow line in rocky, shrub-grown sites. In the far north, where it is plentiful, it inhabits the tundra. It remains faithful to its breeding grounds, descending from the mountain heights into sheltered valleys only during winter. The nest, sparsely lined with grass stems or leaves, is built in May—June in a hollow in the ground beneath a shrub, in heather or in similar places. The female lays 8 to 12 eggs, which she incubates alone for 22 to 26 days. By October the young ptarmigans are full-grown, and families congregate in small groups of 15 to 20 birds. At night they take cover beneath a rock, but also build shelters in the snow. They seek places where larger mammals have cleared the snow, thus providing access to food without effort on their part. In winter the diet consists of seeds and the remains of plants; in spring the ptarmigan nibbles catkins, buds, and, in the Alps for instance, the buds of rhododendrons. In summer it feeds on berries, insects, their larvae and other invertebrates and in autumn relies mainly on various berries. The ptarmigan's summer plumage is chestnut brown with white primaries, its winter dress is all white with dark tail feathers covered with white upper tail coverts. The legs and toes are covered with feathers that prevent the bird from sinking into soft snow. The ptarmigan is a game bird but of no particular consequence.

Length: 34 cm. The male's nuptial dress is mostly grey-brown, the female is coloured reddish brown. *Voice:* The male utters a sound resembling 'kraar'. *Size of Egg:* 41.2 × 29.9 mm on the average.

Golden Eagle
Aquila chrysaetos

Accipitridae

The golden eagle makes its home in rocky locations in Scotland, Scandinavia, Spain, the Alps and Carpathians, and sometimes also in other parts of Europe. This huge bird of prey is generally a resident species, though young individuals roam far afield at the onset of autumn, often to be found in lowland areas and even in the vicinity of large cities. At the end of March or in April the golden eagle builds its large nest, which resembles a huge basket composed of sticks and branches. It is sited, usually, on an inaccessible cliff face, very occasionally in a tree, and is often used for several years. However, within the confines of its territory, to which it remains faithful, it often builds several nests over a period, occupying them successively. The usual clutch of 2 eggs is incubated by the female for 44 to 45 days, the male occasionally relieving her so that she can stretch her wings. The food is hunted by the male, who passes it to the female to give to the nestlings, though when they are older he feeds them himself. The young take to the wing for the first time when they are between 71 and 81 days old, but remain in the company of their parents for a short time after. When they are fully grown they leave their home territory, often travelling great distances. The golden eagle hunts marmots, hares, and other small beasts of prey; sometimes it will kill a young chamois, stray lamb or kid. Young eagles also eat amphibians, reptiles and large insects, and welcome fresh carrion.

Length: 82 cm.
Wing span: 188 to 196 cm. The female is usually larger. The male and female have like plumage.
Voice: A noisy 'kya', and a few whistling notes.
Size of Egg: 70.1—88.9 ×51.0—66.0 mm.

Eurasian Black Vulture

Aegypius monachus

Accipitridae

The black vulture makes its home in the mountain areas of Spain, Sicily and southeastern Europe, though outside the breeding season it may also be seen in Germany, France, Denmark, Poland, Czechoslovakia, and other European countries. Visitors to these latter countries are usually young birds. In the eastern areas this huge bird of prey may be found also in lowland country. The large nest of branches, lined with pieces of animal skins and hair, is built in a tree in the middle of February. The branches used in its construction are broken from a tree by the vulture's strong beak. Both parents take turns incubating the single egg for 55 days. The nestling has a large head, can see as soon as it is born, but the legs are not yet fully developed, its toes being incapable of grasping. The contour feathers do not begin to grow in until the age of one month, and its plumage is not completed until a further month has passed. Both parents feed the young bird, providing half digested food from their crop. The nestling remains in the nest for a long time, usually about three months, before it is capable of flight. The diet consists primarily of carrion, especially the carcasses of larger mammals, the vulture consuming flesh, skin and bone, regurgitating the undigested parts. Only rarely does it hunt live animals, primarily reptiles and amphibians, but if food is very scarce it may even attack a stray lamb. Conspicuous in flight are its long, broad wings with quills spread wide apart.

Length: 103 cm.
Wing span: 265 to 287 cm. The male and female have like plumage.
Weight: 7 to 14 kg.
Voice: Hoarse croaking or wheezing sounds.
Size of Egg: 83.2—107.0 × 56.0—76.0 mm.

Griffon Vulture

Gyps fulvus

Dry, open, rocky sites on mountain slopes and cliffs, less frequently in lowland regions, is where the griffon vulture makes its home. In Europe it occurs in Spain, southwestern France, northern Italy, Switzerland and southeastern Europe. It may also be seen in England, Denmark, Finland and central Europe, but these birds are usually young fledglings. By January adult birds have reached the nesting grounds, where the male courts his partner. The nest of sticks and branches, which the vulture often tears from trees with his beak, is built on an inaccessible cliff ledge in February or March. The hollow in which the egg is laid is lined with the hair and skin of mammals. The single egg is usually white, but may sometimes be spotted brown. It is incubated for 48 to 52 days by both partners. The young bird remains in the nest for about 80 days, during which time the parents feed it half-digested food from the crop. The diet consists chiefly of carcasses of larger mammals, the vultures first ripping out the entrails, but devouring also the muscular tissue and skin. Sometimes they gorge themselves to the extent that they cannot fly, and must then rest for a number of hours to digest their repast. In case of sudden danger they have to regurgitate the food they have consumed before they are able to fly away. They can also go without food for several days without suffering any harm. The griffon vulture attacks live animals only in rare instances, and then only small creatures.

Length: 100 cm.
Wing span: About 240 cm. The male and female have like plumage. Markedly long neck, appearing to be pulled back between the wings in flight.
Voice: A hissing or croaking sound.
Size of Egg: 82.0—106.0 ×64.0—75.0 mm.

Tengmalm's or Boreal Owl

Strigidae

Aegolius funereus

The Tengmalm's owl inhabits central and northern Europe, but its distribution is somewhat irregular. It occurs chiefly in forests, but is to be found also in hill country and lowlands, preferring deep coniferous woods. It is a fairly plentiful species but escapes notice because of its concealed way of life. It often remains during the winter in its breeding grounds, descending from the mountains to the lowlands, where it roams the countryside far and wide. Some birds fly as far as southern France and northern Spain. The courting season begins in March, when one can hear the male's typical voice; sometimes this small owl may be heard also in the autumn. In the middle of April or in May it seeks a nesting cavity, usually an abandoned woodpecker's hole, though it will also welcome a man-made nesting box. It prefers a cavity located at considerable height. The female lays 4 to 6 eggs, which she incubates herself for 25 to 31 days. The young leave the nest at the age of one month and do not return to it, but continue to be fed by the parents either on a branch or in flight. The Tengmalm's owl hunts small rodents such as field mice, mice and dormice, as well as other small mammals and birds. Unlike the little owl, which hunts also in the daytime, the Tengmalm's owl ventures forth only after dusk, remaining concealed in the thick branches of spruce trees or in cavities during the daylight hours. It perches upright on the branch and flies in a direct line. The feet are thickly feathered.

Length: 25 cm.
Wing span: 54 cm. The male and female have like plumage.
Voice: A fairly rapid, repetitious 'poo-poo-poo'.
Size of Egg: 29.0—36.5 ×23.6—28.5 mm.

Dotterel

Charadriidae

Eudromias morinellus

Northern Europe, Scotland and the mountain regions of central Europe are the home of the dotterel, which frequents grass-covered rocky slopes, or the tundra in the far north. In the mountains it is found above the tree line, where it will nest at elevations above 2000 metres. From the end of July to September it wings its way through Europe to its winter quarters in northern Africa or the Middle East, returning by the same route in April—May. At the end of May or the beginning of June it prepares its nest in a hollow in the ground. About 9 centimetres in diameter, it is fairly deep and only sparsely lined with grass stems, leaves and lichens. The female generally lays 3 eggs, but these are incubated only by the male, for a period of 18 to 24 days. When sitting he is so meek that he will often allow himself to be taken up in the hand, and can be returned to the nest without flying off. In northern countries it features in legends as the reincarnation of the Good Spirit, and is mentioned in many books. The young remain in the nest for only one day, after which they follow in the wake of their parents, concealing themselves in the neighbourhood during the day, and sheltered beneath the parents' wings at night. The dotterel is very adroit at moving about in rocky locations. The diet consists chiefly of beetles, flies, worms and small molluscs, and it will occasionally eat green leaflets or small fruits and seeds.

Length: 21.5 cm. The male and female have like plumage.
Voice: Delicate flute-like notes that sound like 'titi-ri-titi-ri'.
Size of Egg: 36.0—46.7 ×26.6—31.5 mm.

BIRDS OF PREY AND THEIR PROTECTION

Europe is the home of some forty species of raptorial birds, of which only nine are regularly seen out of captivity. Unfortunately eagles, vultures and many members of the falcon tribe can no longer be included in this category.

Man is responsible for the almost total disappearance in Europe of the lammergeyer or bearded vulture *(Gypaetus barbatus)*. At one time it was a regular nester in the German Alps, and the last specimen living there was shot in 1855. Up to 1866 the bearded vulture also nested in the Swiss Alps, but it was not seen again until 1955, almost a hundred years later, when it showed up in the Salzkammergut in Austria. Records of its nesting in the Carpathians date from as late as 1935, but since then there has been no further sign of the bird. The bearded vulture lays one or at most two eggs, and the bird's propagation is very slow in natural conditions. If just one of a pair of nesting birds is shot, the other usually abandons the area and seeks a new site. Sometimes it may take several years before it finds a new mate capable of having young, for members of this species take four to five years to reach maturity.

Vultures, too, are becoming increasingly rare in Europe and deserve total protection, if for no other reason than that they feed mainly on carrion.

The treatment of some birds of prey like the goshawk is often a subject of dispute between conservation groups and game-keepers. It is true that the goshawk preys mostly on birds, but these are mainly corvine birds, which cause much damage to small songsters and game birds because of their fondness for their eggs. Naturally, the goshawk's victims also include useful birds as well as game birds and domestic pigeons. In pheasant preserves where these game birds are bred they can cause serious depletion of the young. However, there is an equally strong argument in favour of protecting the goshawk. Experience has shown that wherever it has been exterminated jays, crows and magpies have multiplied in such numbers that they have caused far greater damage to wildlife than that wreaked by several goshawk families. Furthermore, the goshawk is a resident bird and its young remain in the vicinity of their territory, usually settling within sixty kilometres of the nest where they were reared. This makes it possible to keep a check on the goshawk population in a given territory and gamekeepers should resort to limiting the bird's number only after very careful consideration or in the case of overpopulation.

Protection, at least in part, should also be given to the most common of small predators, the sparrow hawk, which preys chiefly on the house sparrow, a generally acknowledged pest. Although its victims include a great many other birds, the sparrow hawk plays an important role in the regulation of ecological balance except in the case of overpopulation.

Absolute protection throughout the year should be afforded the common buzzard, because it feeds chiefly on fieldmice, mice and other harmful rodents, including hamsters and insects. Sometimes, of course, its victims are creatures such as the partridge and pheasant, which are useful to man. There have, in fact, been instances of individual buzzards which fed only on young pheasants, but these occasions are rare. Detailed analyses have been made of the stomach contents of buzzards throughout the whole of Europe and these have shown that mice and fieldmice comprise a full 96.3 per cent of their diet; 3.7 per cent consisted of wild game, mostly birds that were weakened or diseased. At times of mice overpopulation, these creatures comprise up to 88 per cent of the buzzard's diet.

The honey buzzard, which resembles the common buzzard but has longer wings, is another raptor that deserves full protection as it is by no means an abundant species. It feeds mainly on the larvae of wasps and only occasionally captures a vertebrate.

Among those birds which require protection the whole year round are members of the falcon tribe. The saker falcon, for example, one of the largest of the family, used to nest in comparative abundance in central Europe, but today it occurs only in eastern Europe with any regularity. The disappearance of the saker falcon from central Europe in the nineteenth century was caused primarily by collectors who shot adult birds for ornithological exhibits, and by those who took the eggs from their nests.

The peregrine falcon, though widespread throughout Europe, is elsewhere becoming rare. In some places it was hunted mercilessly to prevent it from killing off domestic pigeons, and its former nesting grounds have become depleted. It is true that the peregrine hunts birds, and pigeons head the list, but others include starlings, magpies, crows and rooks, and in some places these latter species make up as much as 85 per cent of its diet. In some areas it has become unpopular because it occasionally catches a partridge or pheasant. One thing is certain, however; by catching crows and other corvine birds which can cause considerable damage, the peregrine saves quite a number of useful as well as game birds. Furthermore, when many falcons migrate southwest in the autumn they feast on pigeons which have reverted to the wild state and which are found in abundance in large cities. These 'city' pigeons have a tendency to overmultiply and are causing untold damage with their droppings to old and treasured buildings and houses. Thus, in view of the fact that the peregrine is becoming a truly rare bird, it should be protected by all possible measures wherever it is still found.

The small hobby, though harmless, was mercilessly killed by hunters and in many places exterminated completely. It is only found in large numbers where people know its mode of life and afford it some protection. The hobby feeds on insects and small birds, which it catches on the wing, and only rarely captures a small mammal. The hobby should, therefore, be protected, not only because it poses no threat to husbandry but, above all, because it is becoming a comparatively rare species.

The smallest European falcon, the merlin, is a bird of the north and occasionally nests in northern Britain. In central and western Europe it is known only as a winter guest. It, too, deserves protection for it hunts only insects and small birds like the sparrow.

The Eurasian kestrel, probably the most common European raptor of the *Falconidae* family, is renowned for its usefulness and is therefore protected wherever it is found.

The rapid disappearance of eagles, harriers, kites and other kinds of European predators indicated an indisputable need to protect and preserve the species. Extermination of the species should no longer be condoned, neither out of ignorance nor to further man's own narrow and selfish interests. Man has already caused irreparable damage and should now endeavour, as far as possible, to right the wrongs of his predecessors and to prevent further destruction of his environment, of which all animal life is a part.

THE HISTORY OF FALCONRY

According to historical records birds of prey, especially falcons, have been used by man for hunting since ancient times. As early as circa 400 B.C. the Indians trained these birds, especially saker falcons, and there is an account of falcons being used for hunting by the men of Thrace in the year 75 A.D. Falconry in Rome dates from 480 A.D. The new sport soon became widespread and even Church dignitaries began to show an interest in it.

About 800 A.D. Charlemagne issued a decree pertaining to trained hawks and falcons, and the following excerpt shows the high regard in which these birds were held: 'Whoever steals or traps a goshawk that hunts cranes must return same plus six shillings, and three shillings for a falcon that catches birds on the wing. Whoever steals or kills a sparrow hawk or other bird of prey borne on the wrist, must replace it in kind and pay one shilling'.

At the courts of emperors, kings and feudal lords countless falconers were employed, and many a chief falconer was raised to the ranks of the nobility for his services. In many countries there were schools of falconry that gained a world-wide reputation. Falcons trained there were often more highly prized than gold or other treasures, as the following example indicates. At the Battle of Nicopolis, in 1396, the Turkish Sultan Baiasid I captured the Duke of Nevers and many other nobles, refusing to accept ransom of any kind. However, when the Duke of Burgundy, father of the Duke of Nevers, sent a gift of twelve white falcons, the Sultan released all his French prisoners.

Many rulers issued strict laws for the protection of birds of prey. Thus, Edward III of England even made the theft of a goshawk punishable by death, and the sentence for anyone who stole the eggs from a goshawk's nest was imprisonment for a year and a day. At that time goshawks still nested in England, but today nesting birds are no longer found there. In other countries, too, maximum punishments were laid down by law for the protection of falcons. In Iceland, for example, until 1752 the punishment for killing a falcon was death.

Falconer's guilds and schools of falconry thrived. Falkenwerth in Flanders, as its name suggests, was a centre of falconry which maintained a considerable reputation for centuries. Its falconers journeyed to Norway and Iceland in search of white falcons, but in Iceland only the local inhabitants were allowed to hunt these birds, and, even then, only by special permit. All captured birds had to be delivered to the 'grand' falconer of the King of Denmark. The Dutch, too, famous for their mastery in catching and training falcons, played an important part in the history of falconry and Charles V founded a falconers' guild in Holland in 1539.

The white falcon of Iceland, Norway and northern Siberia was a very highly valued bird. It was generally shipped by boat from Iceland to Copenhagen, being fed en route with the flesh of rams, taken aboard especially for this purpose.

Russia, too, had its schools of falconry. In the fourteenth century, when this sport became very widespread, falconers journeyed as far as the Pechora River and Novaya Zemlya to hunt falcons. In the sixteenth century the annual catch often comprised about a hundred of these birds, many of which served as diplomatic gifts. Regular shipments of hunting birds were sent to England, Poland, Denmark, Turkey, the Crimea and Persia. The Shahs of Persia considered hunting falcons as gifts of such great value that, in return, they often promised to provide Russian princes with military aid against their adversaries.

Records of falconry in the Orient, dating back even further in time than those in Europe, are worthy of note. In fact, falconry probably had its origins in Asia, for falconers are known to have existed more than 3,600 years ago in Babylonia, as shown by sculptured reliefs at the ruins of Chorsabad. In China, falconry was known as early as 2,205 B.C.

The sport was also very popular in Persia where, in the year 1681, the Shah had at his court more than eight hundred falcons trained to hunt geese, cranes and herons, as well as foxes, antelopes and wild boars.

The Mongols, Kirghizes and Bashkirs even trained the golden eagle and lesser spotted eagle to hunt foxes and wolves, and hunting on horseback with large eagles remains a popular sport of native hunters to this day.

In the nineteenth century the popularity of falconry began to wane, though it continued in England, Holland and to some extent also in France, Germany and Russia. Today England, Holland, Germany and Hungary are the only countries where sportsmen hunt regularly with birds, though in recent years falconry groups or societies have been founded in other parts of Europe as well.

Hunting falcons were usually captured from mid-September on, the hunting season lasting for about three weeks. In Holland, for example, during such a period, the falconer and his assistants would catch some twelve to fifteen falcons, generally in trap baskets with live pigeons as bait. Falconers in Iceland concentrated on young, recently fledged birds, since these were best suited for training. Less frequent was the practice of taking birds from the nest, for young falcons that had not yet learned to hunt their own prey were not so easily trained.

The equipment used for training falcons consists of a hood to cover the bird's eyes, a short strap, and a long strap measuring about two metres in length, which is fastened to a leather ring around the bird's foot. Some form of decoy and thick leather gauntlets are also required.

Firstly the bird has to become accustomed to the trainer who feeds it from his hand. Then the falconer covers the bird's head with the hood, fastens the bird to the short strap and lets it fast for twenty-four hours. He then lifts the bird with his gloved hand, removes the hood and offers it some food. If the bird refuses to eat the procedure is repeated for another twenty-four hours, and if necessary for five days in succession. Even then, the bird is only given food by the falconer, either in the aviary or tied to his hand.

After the bird has learned to take the meat from the falconer's hand, it passes to the next step in its training programme. The falconer fastens the bird to the long strap, removes the hood and throws a dead pigeon, stuffed crow or similar bait into the air, whereupon the bird flies up after the prey. The falconer allows it to eat a small piece of the 'victim's' flesh, but then it is immediately made to eat meat again from the falconer's hand. This procedure is repeated a number of times, and then the bird is sent after its prey on the long strap and taught to return at the sight of the decoy. The decoy is an egg-shaped object, with a few wing quills attached, and is made so that it can easily be seen from a distance. The decoy is waved above the falconer's head to bring the bird back to him when it is out hunting. On its return the bird is rewarded with food from the falconer's hand so that it always feels bound to man.

The birds most widely used for this purpose were the gyrfalcon *(Falco rusticolus)*, which is found in both grey and white varieties, the white of the species being the most highly valued; the saker falcon *(Falco cherrug)* of central Europe and the East; the peregrine falcon *(Falco peregrinus)*, and the lanner falcon *(Falco biarmicus)* of southern Italy, Sicily, Cyprus, Greece and northwest Africa. Of the smaller species the hobby *(Falco subbuteo)* and merlin *(Falco columbarius)* were most popular with ladies of the court. Catherine, Empress of Russia, had a great number of merlins trained to hunt. In the Orient other members of the falcon tribe were used for this purpose: namely the goshawk *(Accipiter gentilis)* and the smaller sparrow hawk *(Accipiter nisus)*. The golden eagle *(Aquila chrysaetos)* and the imperial eagle *(Aquila heliaca)* were particularly favoured in eastern countries.

To prevent further decimation of rare birds of prey only those birds like the goshawk, which are still found in relative abundance, should be used for this sport.

OWLS AND THEIR PROTECTION

From ancient times the owl was regarded as the symbol of wisdom, and consequently was afforded protection. But in many parts of Europe during the Middle Ages it became associated with witchcraft and the forces of evil, and has been depicted thus in countless fairy tales. This accounts for the widespread belief that the cry of the little owl, attracted by a light in a window, foretells death in the house. Such beliefs soon resulted in owls being pursued without mercy in many places. Even today it is not uncommon to come across people who shoot owls or destroy their nests.

Owls have been wonderfully equipped by nature for hunting at night. Unlike other birds, their eyes are not located at the sides of the head but face forward, thus making their range of vision only about 160°. However, this is compensated by the owl's ability to twist its head around a full 270°. The eye is also unusually large, with a wide lens and very contractile iris that regulates the penetration of light, allowing in more at night and less by day. The owl can thus see remarkably well under practically all circumstances. In addition, the eye is able to focus quickly on small objects, even at great distances, allowing the bird to sight a small mouse at a range of several tens of metres. Closure of its eye is also different from that of other birds, in that the upper, instead of the lower lid, closes. In addition they also have a second membraneous eyelid that slides from the inner to the outer corner of the eye.

Owls have an excellently developed sense of hearing, which helps them to locate their prey even in total darkness. Many owls have enlarged feathers round the ears or round the perimeter of the head, which enable them to catch the slightest sound; that is why the owl turns its face towards a sound and is able to pinpoint the position of its prey, which it then proceeds to catch without a sound.

Silent flight is a typical feature of owls. Once airborne, an owl seems more like a shadow, and the swish of its feathers cannot be heard. The reason for this is that its plumage is soft and fluffy, and the surface of the wing and tail feathers is covered with fine down. The toes, too, have a coating of fine down which deadens any sound as the bird alights on a branch. In the young bird the first powder-down plumage is replaced by a coat of semi-down and normal feathers are acquired when the bird begins to fly. It is often possible to see baby owls which are incapable of flight and which still have remains of their semi-down coat.

Owls are predators in the main, though they have little in common with the true birds of prey and are more closely related to the nightjar. They primarily hunt a variety of vertebrates as well as insects and sometimes crustaceans. Unlike true birds of prey, which first pluck their victims clean and then tear off pieces of flesh, owls swallow large pieces or entire small animals, without any preparation. Larger owls, such as the Ural owl and long-eared owl, swallow beetles, mice and fieldmice whole. The indigestible parts — feathers, hairs, bones and hard insect covers — are regurgitated in solid lumps that look as if they have been pressed. If these are carefully separated they will be found to contain entire skulls of fieldmice, mice and birds and the *elytra* and legs of beetles and other insects. This makes it possible to determine not only the quantity but also the kind of food cosumed by the owl.

Since owls do not possess a crop in which to conserve a store of food, they often bring to their nest or hide more than they are able to consume in a day. When the female is incubating, the male often brings dozens of fieldmice or other small animals, to serve as a reserve supply in case the ensuing days should be lean ones.

Europe is the home of fourteen species of owls, most of them nocturnal birds. The food they live on is the subject of study by countless ornithologists. They have found that the diet of the tawny owl, one of the most common of the European owls, consists mainly of fieldmice and mice. In the case of some individual owls, birds make up about 14 per cent of the diet; of this half are sparrows, and the other half is made up of greenfinches, warblers, starlings and blackbirds. These are birds which are normally found in abundance. If cockchafers are in large supply a great part of the owls' food will be made up of these harmful pests.

Another common species, the long-eared owl, feeds largely on small rodents, especially in years when there is an over-population of mice. Otherwise, the chief food is again the house sparrow, almost 67 per cent, followed by the greenfinch, Eurasian tree sparrow and blackbird, in other words birds that are more or less harmful. Only in three recorded instances was the food consumed found to contain a partridge. When cockchafers are in abundance these also represent a major part of the long-eared owl's diet.

In the case of the barn owl, small rodents, fieldmice and mice average about 69 per cent of the diet, shrews 25 per cent, birds only 3 per cent and bats, amphibians and larger mammals make up the remainder. In years of 'mouse' overpopulation the share of these rodents in this owl's diet has been recorded as being as high as 95.7 per cent.

The little owl also feeds mainly on fieldmice and mice, which together comprises usually 76 per cent and occasionally as much as 100 per cent of the bird's diet. In the summer months insects make up a large proportion, but the little owl also hunts to a lesser extent shrews and small birds, mainly starlings, followed by house sparrows, blackbirds and thrushes, i.e. birds that are very plentiful and which, in some areas, have overmultiplied in recent years.

The above four species of owls are very common in Europe. Other types are much more rare, and some occur only sporadically. These, too, feed mostly on a variety of rodents and insects.

The Eurasian eagle owl, the largest of the European species, is one of a number of owls that were almost on the brink of extinction in Europe and which now, thanks to stricter rules governing their protection, have again increased in number. Even though it often feeds on wild game such as hare, rabbit, pheasant and wild duck, the greater part of the eagle owl's diet is made up of fieldmice and mice, with hedgehogs and wild rabbits following closely behind. Among birds which it eats partridges and moorhens head the list, followed by large numbers of hooded crows and several birds of prey — buzzards, kestrels, falcons and even other species of owls. In lake regions it feeds on various water birds and waders. Although the Eurasian eagle owl's victims may occasionally be animals which serve a useful natural purpose, it should be given the fullest protection, not only because it is a rare species, but also because it generally kills weak or diseased animals, thus helping to maintain a balanced ecology.

Even today in some places hunters and gamekeepers take the young from the eagle owl's nest and use them as bait to attract crows and predators, which are known for their hatred of owls and, in particular, of their greatest enemy, the eagle owl. They can spot it from a great distance and the instant they do so they attack without delay. Hunters take advantage of this fact, using an eagle owl as bait, fastened to a perch by leather thongs. The hunter then conceals himself in a hide with a good view of his bait and waits with his gun cocked. The owl generally catches sight of the approaching predator while it is still some way off, and begins to rattle its bill. It often jumps from the perch to the ground, where it lies down on its back and spreads its talons in readiness to ward off the enemy. This unsporting method of hunting is now forbidden in many European countries, because it is necessary to protect both the eagle owl and the birds of prey. Hunters sometimes shoot a rare or useful predator.

Owls should be given protection throughout the whole year, and there are many ways in which the ordinary layman can help them during the nesting period. This applies especially to those that nest in cavities such as the tawny owl, who would benefit greatly from a nest box. This is easily constructed and should be approx. 30 centimetres wide by 40 centimetres high, with an entrance hole 13 centimetres square located in one of the upper corners. The box should be fastened to a tree about 6 to 8 metres above the ground and positioned preferably at the edge of a wood so that the owl can hunt in the surrounding fields.

For the little owl and Tengmalm's owl, the nest box should be about 20 centimetres wide and 35 centimetres high and the width of the entrance hole about 9 centimetres. Small owls, such as the pygmy, will even make use of a sparrow's nestbox, but prefer one made from a piece of hollowed-out tree trunk. This should be about 30 centimetres high, with an entrance hole about 5 centimetres across, and it should be hung 4 to 8 metres above the ground.

GAME BIRDS OF THE WOODLANDS

At the beginning of this century birds were still being hunted more or less without limitations the world over. This led to the complete extinction of some species. The fate of the dodo *(Raphus cucullatus)* of Mauritius, which became extinct in the late seventeenth century is a familiar one. North America was once inhabited by millions of passenger pigeons *(Ectopistes migratorius)*, but the last was captured in 1907. Until recently many songbirds could be bought in the marketplaces of large cities, and in Italy these small birds were captured in nets on a large scale.

The formation of hunting associations and conservation groups led to a marked restriction of the unlicensed shooting of birds, but even more important has been the signing of international agreements to ensure the protection of birds, in some cases entirely prohibiting the hunting of certain species.

The number of game bird species has consequently become constant, even though this may vary in individual countries of Europe according to given circumstances. Today, for example, the hazel hen is a protected species in central Europe, where it is considered a rare bird, yet in northern Europe it is a common game bird of the woods. Certain members of the thrush tribe were numbered among typical game birds in the past, and still are in many parts of Europe, the fieldfare being considered a particular delicacy.

Pigeons are still very popular game birds and their meat is considered good and palatable. One example is the stock dove, which is protected in some countries because of its scarcity. Less commonly hunted is the turtle dove, even though it is quite common in some places.

Hunting the woodcock is usually an unforgettable experience for most sportsmen and this takes place in the open season, in spring, when the birds return from their winter quarters. The woodcocks fly shortly after sunset, winging their way close above treetops and clearings, along the edges of forests and down the valleys of streams and rivers, and it is here that the hunter lies in wait for the birds. The shooting of woodcocks, however, should only be permitted in the autumn and not in spring, which is a time for nesting when the bird needs peace and quiet.

The commonest game birds are the fowl-like species, most of which are not migratory. Hunters can play an active role in the nesting ecology and ensure their propagation, as in the case of pheasants and partridges, with semi-wild breeds.

The pheasant is the most commonly hunted game bird today. Thousands of these birds are sold in shops in the autumn and winter months and add variety to the daily diet, their meat being considered a real delicacy. The bird is hunted in the autumn and large numbers of sportsmen take part in organized shoots, which involve the use of beaters and hunting dogs to flush the birds and drive them towards the guns. In some countries, pheasants are bred artificially in aviaries and delivered directly from there to the shops.

Among game birds of the gallinaceous species members of the grouse tribe are worthy of note. The hazel hen *(Tetrastes bonasia)*, which weighs about 350—450 grammes, is today protected in most parts of central Europe, though in former times it was a popular delicacy. Its specific Latin name is derived from the words *bona asa*, which roughly translated mean something like 'good roast'.

The black grouse, which weighs as much as 1.5 kilograms, is larger and more common. The lyre-shaped tail feathers of the male are used as trophies to adorn the hats of fortunate hunters. The taiga of northern Europe and Asia represents its main area of distribution; it is found less frequently in central Europe. The black grouse is hunted in early spring, during its courting season and the occasion when the male performs his strange courtship display. As each cock has claim to several hens there is no danger of their numbers being depleted by shooting the males. In the appropriate season the black grouse performs its courtship antics together with other males at special display territories. Those who wish to observe this procedure must arrive very early, usually before sunrise. The dancing grounds are generally situated in forest clearings, or in a meadow or field near a wood. The performance begins with loud calls; then the cocks hop up and down, flutter their wings, spread their fan-shaped tails and stretch their necks. This is followed by their running round in a circle at increasing speed, uttering burbling sounds. Finally the cocks face each other, head on, and engage in fierce combat, though as a rule they cause each other little harm. These courtship antics last until sunrise, when the hens arrive on the scene to be led off by the bravest of the males.

One of the most exciting sports is hunting the capercaillie, largest of the European grouse, the male weighing as much as 6 kilograms and the hen 2.5—3 kilograms. Its main area of distribution is northern Europe and Asia; in central Europe and Scotland it is fairly common, but only in areas with extensive forests near to mountains. The hunter usually sets out alone after the so-called 'King of the Woods', probably because a companion might scare this extremely shy bird. The cock usually starts his courtship display while it is still dark, and this takes place on a thick horizontal branch high up in the treetops. The courting 'serenade' begins with a noise resembling two wooden sticks being struck against each other, five to fifteen times in succession. This is followed by short, soft popping noises, ending with a loud pop and followed by three buzzing sounds. This is the cue for the hunter to approach his prey, for at this particular moment the serenader is 'blind' and 'deaf' to all around him; his eyes are closed tight and the base of the lower beak is pressed closely against his eardrums. The cock will not necessarily remain in one spot during this display, but often runs back and forth along the branch or skips from one branch to another. As dawn breaks he descends to the ground, where he has marked out his special territory, and sometimes engages in fierce combat with his rivals, so violent that occasionally one of them is killed. The victor is then surrounded by hens, which fly down from the treetops, and there are usually several of them to each cock.

Game birds also include other fowl-like species such as the rock partridge and ptarmigan.

BIRDS INTRODUCED
FROM OTHER COUNTRIES

For centuries man has tried to adopt and acclimatize new species of game, including game birds. Introducing game birds to a foreign country does, of course, present a number of difficulties, the main one being that they are capable of flight and can thus escape easily. Therefore only those species that are poor fliers or completely incapable of flight can be released in the wild when introduced to new environments. Experience has proved that some of the gallinaceous species best fulfil these requirements.

The one which has best acclimatized itself to different conditions in widely-spread areas of the world has been the common pheasant *(Phasianus colchicus)*, indigenous in many varieties to central, east and southeast Asia. About 1260 B.C. a Greek expedition to Colchis, a region on the eastern coast of the Black Sea, discovered on the banks of the River Phasis an unusual bird which, because of its habitat, they named *Phasianus ornis*. At a later date this pheasant was given the specific scientific name *colchicus*, referring to its place of origin. The Greeks succeeded in capturing several live birds which they took back to Greece from where, in due course, the pheasant became known to the Romans. Some time around the year 900 A.D. the pheasant was brought to Great Britain, where it soon became very popular and, as a result, began to be bred in special pheasant preserves. It was probably introduced into central Europe in the eleventh century, where it was bred in Bohemia on lands belonging to monasteries. Thereafter, the pheasant soon became widespread, being considered a common game bird from the twelfth century on. In Bohemia, as in England, pheasants began to be bred on a large scale and soon became the favourite target of sportsmen.

The demand for pheasants increased similarly in other European countries, and it later became known as the English pheasant or Bohemian pheasant, depending on its source of origin.

For a long time the only pheasant bred in Europe was the species from Colchis. But in 1742, with the spread of ocean shipping and more rapid transit round the world, the subspecies *Phasianus colchicus torquatus*, the ring-necked pheasant, so called because of the white ring around its neck, found its way from China to England, where it interbred with the common pheasant. The ring-necked pheasant also found its way to other parts of Europe, in time replacing the original stock wherever it was introduced, or else cross-breeding with it to produce hybrids. Later still, another subspecies was introduced into Europe, namely *Phasianus colchicus mongolicus*. All these various races intermingled, and today one would be hard put to find typical representatives of certain subspecies amongst European pheasants. In consequence the German name *Jagdfasan* (game pheasant) is perhaps the most fitting for these European hybrids.

The common pheasant has become practically extinct in its native home in Transcaucasia, and the few birds still to be found there are strictly protected by law. The reasons why it began to die out are not yet fully understood. It is certain, however, that the original European breed of *Phasianus colchicus* is a thing of the past. Nevertheless, the pheasant is here to stay and is one of the leading game birds in many European countries.

In 1840 another species, the green pheasant *(Phasianus versicolor)* was brought to Amsterdam, from Japan. The existing dark mutation, *Phasianus colchicus* var. *tenebrosus*, is probably the result of cross-breeding between the green and the originally-introduced pheasant from Colchis. Today even this mutation is rarely seen in the wild, for it, too, has disappeared as a result of cross-breeding.

Another pheasant bred with intermittent success in large game preserves is the Reeves's pheasant *(Syrmaticus reevesi)*, found in the wooded hills of central China. To see the magnificently coloured cock, with tail feathers sometimes more than 1.5 metres long, is an unforgettable experience.

The golden pheasant *(Chrysolophus pictus)*, first brought to England from the mountainous areas of central China in 1740, was also introduced experimentally into some preserves but with little success. The same applies to the related Lady Amherst pheasant *(Chrysolophus amherstiae)*, which is found in the mountains of southeast Tibet and southwest China, where it occurs at elevations of up to 4000 metres. The cock of this species is also brightly coloured and in Europe, where the vegetation is not as dense and does not provide sufficient cover, it soon falls victim to birds of prey and other predators.

Another gallinaceous bird which was introduced more recently in some parts of central Europe is the rock partridge *(Alectoris graeca)*, a native of the high mountain regions of central China and Tibet and found also in the Alps and Pyrenees. Although a hardy bird (it occurs at elevations as high as 5000 metres), its acclimatization in new territories has not met with any particular success to date.

The common or wild turkey *(Meleagris gallopavo)* was also introduced as an experiment. It is a native of America, where it inhabits the woodlands and scrubs in Mexico and the southeastern United States. When Columbus discovered America the wild turkey was widespread and had already been domesticated by the Indians of Central America. The Spanish conquistador, Hernando Cortez, found flocks numbering thousands of turkey hens in the courtyards of Montezuma's palace. Most probably it was the Spaniards who first brought these birds to Europe in 1498, though according to other sources John Cabot brought two turkeys to Henry VII of England a year earlier. From Spain these birds spread throughout Europe and became most common in England, where, however, the prime interest lay in breeding them as domesticated fowl. In the late nineteenth and early twentieth century, turkeys captured in the wild were brought to many parts of Europe, where they were placed in large game preserves and, in isolated instances, lived in the wild in deciduous woods. The experimental introduction of wild turkeys has also been carried out elsewhere in Europe.

The meat of the wild turkey (the male can weigh up to 15 kg) is more tasty than that of the domesticated bird and, consequently, great efforts are being made to breed it for hunting purposes. Its acclimatization to European conditions, however, has not met with great success. Even though adult birds are very hardy and thrive at lower elevations, the chicks are extremely intolerant of the more rugged European climate, especially the cold damp of the spring months. Furthermore, these birds are large and conspicuous and become easy prey to foxes and, to add to the difficulties, the turkey is careless during the nesting period and is apt to wander off. Another reason why the wild turkey has not become widespread on the Continent is because it must be well fed during the winter months and is therefore a costly breeding proposition.

In conclusion, it may be said that of all the attempts to acclimatize new species of birds, complete success has been attained only in the case of the common pheasant. This has become one of the most widespread birds in Europe and ranges as far north as southern Scandinavia.

BIBLIOGRAPHY

Austin, O. L.: *Birds of the World*. London, 1963.

Bannerman, D. A.: *The Birds of the British Isles*. Edinburgh, 1953—63.

Benson, S. V.: *The Observer's Book of British Birds*. London, 1937.

Bruun, B. and Singer, A.: *The Hamlyn Guide to Birds of Britain and Europe*. London, 1970.

Dementiev, G. P., et al.: *Birds of the USSR*. In Russian. Moscow, 1951—54.

Grassé, O.: *Traité de Zoologie, vol. XV. Oiseaux*. Paris, 1950.

Heinroth, O. et M.: *Die Vögel Mitteleuropas*. Frankfurt a. M., 1966—68.

Jespersen, P.: *Migration of Birds*. London, 1950.

Lincoln, F.: *Migrating of Birds*. London, 1950.

Peterson, R. T., Mounfort, G., Hollom, P. A.: *Birds of Britain and Europe*. London, 1971.

Rudebeck, G.: *Studies of Bird Migration*. London, 1950.

Schütz, E.: *Vom Vogelzug*. Frankfurt am Main, 1952.

Thomson, A.: *A New Dictionary of Birds*. London and Edinburgh, 1964.

Van Ijzendoorn, A. L.: *The Breeding Birds of the Netherlands*. Leiden, 1950.

Voous, K. K.: *Atlas of European Birds*. London, 1960.

Witherby, H. F.: *The Handbook of British Birds*. London, 1938—41.

INDEX OF COMMON NAMES